Ravenscourt
B·O·O·K·S
Teacher's Guide

Express Yourself

Books 1-8

Thousand-Mile Words
They Landed One Night
Bidding on the Past
Blues King: The Story of B. B. King
Sports Superstars
Art for All!
The Last Leaf and The Gift
Oliver Twist

McGraw Hill SRA

Columbus, OH

SRAonline.com

McGraw Hill SRA

Copyright © 2008 by SRA/McGraw-Hill.

All rights reserved. No part of this publication may be reproduced or distributed in any form or by any means, or stored in a database or retrieval system, without the prior written consent of The McGraw-Hill Companies, Inc., including, but not limited to, network storage or transmission, or broadcast for distance learning.

Printed in the United States of America.

Send all inquiries to this address:
SRA/McGraw-Hill
4400 Easton Commons
Columbus, OH 43219

ISBN: 978-0-07-611314-9
MHID: 0-07-611314-0

2 3 4 5 6 7 8 9 MAL 13 12 11 10 09 08 07

The **McGraw·Hill** Companies

Table of Contents

Ravenscourt Books 1
Reading and Fluency 2
Using *Ravenscourt Books* 3
Individual Progress Chart 8
Fluency Graph 9
Book Summaries 10
Thousand-Mile Words 12
   Answer Key 22
They Landed One Night 24
   Answer Key 34
Bidding on the Past 36
   Answer Key 46
Blues King: The Story of B. B. King 48
   Answer Key 58
Sports Superstars 60
   Answer Key 70
Art for All! 72
   Answer Key 82
The Last Leaf and The Gift 84
   Answer Key 94
Oliver Twist 96
   Answer Key 106
Graphic Organizers 108

Ravenscourt Books

Placing Students

Written for middle school to young adult readers, *Ravenscourt Books* provides materials and activities for enhancing the comprehension and fluency of struggling readers. Each of these fiction and nonfiction selections is

- organized within themes that are both engaging and informative.
- built to provide students with additional opportunities to read independently.
- designed to provide frequent opportunities for reading to improve fluency and overall reading achievement.

Some teachers have found these selections align with the independent reading levels of students in the *Corrective Reading* program. Use the chart below to place your students in the appropriate set of *Ravenscourt Readers*.

	For students who have successfully completed	Reading level	Page count (average number of words per book)
Getting Started	Corrective Reading Decoding A*	1	28 (800)
Discovery	Corrective Reading Comprehension A*	2	28 (1,800)
Anything's Possible	Corrective Reading Decoding B1*	2	28 (1,800)
The Unexpected	Corrective Reading Comprehension B1*	2	28 (1,800)
Express Yourself	Corrective Reading Decoding B2*	3	44 (4,200)
Overcoming Adversity	Corrective Reading Comprehension B2*	3	44 (4,200)
Moving Forward	Corrective Reading Decoding C* Lesson 60	5	60 (7,500)
Reaching Goals	Corrective Reading Comprehension C* Lesson 60	5	60 (7,500)

*or have attained comparable skills

Components

The **Using *Ravenscourt Books*** section explains how to incorporate these components into an effective supplemental reading program.

Chapter Books
- Include eight age-appropriate books in each set
- Feature fiction, nonfiction, and retold classics
- Present additional practice for essential vocabulary and decoding skills
- Provide fast-moving story lines for independent reading

Fluency Audio CDs
- Model pronunciation, phrasing, intonation, and expression
- Assist students in improving their oral-reading fluency

Evaluation and Tracking Software
- Motivates students by delivering activities electronically
- Scores, records, and tracks student progress

Teacher's Guides
- Outline ways to use the series in your classroom
- Include comprehension activities, word lists, and fluency practice
- Provide prereading activities and postreading writing activities
- Address reading and language arts standards

Online Support

Go to **SRAonline.com** and click on *Ravenscourt Books* for additional support and materials.

Express Yourself

Reading and Fluency

Reading

Reading is not simply decoding or word recognition; it is understanding the text. Students who read slowly or hesitantly are not able to concentrate on meaning.

Fluency

Fluency bridges the gap between decoding and comprehension and characterizes proficient reading. Increased oral-reading fluency improves reading comprehension.

Fluent and Nonfluent Readers

The chart below presents an easy way to compare fluent and nonfluent readers. If students have several of the listed characteristics of nonfluent readers, refer to the sections on *Assessing Fluency* and *Fluency Practice* in the **Using *Ravenscourt Books*** section that begins on page 3.

A Fluent Reader	A Nonfluent Reader
Reads words accurately	Reads with omissions, pauses, mispronunciations, insertions, and substitutions
Decodes automatically	Reverses word order
Reads smoothly	Reads word-by-word, focusing on words
Reads at an appropriate rate	Reads slowly, hesitantly
Reads with expression and phrasing	Reads without expression; ignores punctuation
Reads with understanding of text	Reads with limited comprehension
Reads so text sounds like speech	Reads without natural intonation

Oral-Reading Fluency

Oral-reading fluency is the ability to read accurately, at an appropriate rate, and with good expression and phrasing. The foundation for oral-reading fluency is automatic word recognition and extensive practice with materials that are easy for the students to read.

Oral-reading fluency develops as a result of multiple opportunities to practice reading successfully. The primary strategy for developing oral-reading fluency is to provide extensive and frequent opportunities for students to read text with high levels of accuracy. This means that selected passages should be ones the students are able to read with at least 95 percent accuracy.

Repeated and monitored oral reading is an effective intervention strategy for students who do not read fluently. By reading the same passage a number of times, students become familiar with the words it contains and recognize the words automatically. This improves reading fluency and overall reading achievement. It also builds confidence and motivation—particularly when students chart their progress.

The minimum target oral-reading fluency rate is 60 *words read correctly per minute* (wcpm) for **Getting Started** and **Discovery,** 90 wcpm for **Anything's Possible** and **The Unexpected,** 130 wcpm for **Express Yourself** and **Overcoming Adversity,** and 150 wcpm for **Moving Forward** and **Reaching Goals.**

How to assess fluency, how to set realistic target rates, and how to practice fluency will be discussed in greater detail in the **Using *Ravenscourt Books*** section.

Using *Ravenscourt Books*

Grouping

Students who have completed *Decoding B2* will have mastered the decoding skills and vocabulary necessary to independently read the stories in **Express Yourself.**

Ravenscourt Books may be taught to the whole class, small groups, or pairs. Assign each student to a partner. Partners can do paired readings for fluency practice. The partners will read the same story at the same time. *Ravenscourt Books* may also be used for individual student reading.

Scheduling

Ravenscourt Books is intended to be used as a supplement to your core program and should be scheduled in addition to the regular lessons. Times to use the books include

- reading and language arts blocks,
- before- and after-school programs,
- summer school,
- and out-of-school reading with parental support.

A Suggested Lesson Plan for *Ravenscourt Books*

Part 1	1) Introduce the series, and help students select a book. 2) Assess students' initial oral-reading fluency by completing a "cold read" of one of the book's fluency passages. The **Fluency Passage** section can be found after the **Thinking and Writing** section for each book. (See *Assessing Fluency* on page 4.) 3) Have students complete the **Building Background** activities.
Part 2	1) Preteach the unfamiliar words for the first chapter in the **Word Lists** section of the *Teacher's Guide* for each book. 2) Have students read the title of the first chapter aloud. 3) Have students listen to a fluent reader read the first chapter as they follow along with the text. 4) Have student pairs take turns reading the chapter again. 5) Have students take the **Chapter Quiz.** 6) Have some students do repeated readings to improve oral-reading fluency. 7) Repeat Part 2 for subsequent chapters.
Part 3	1) Have students complete the **Thinking and Writing** section. 2) Take fluency scores, using the same fluency passage used in Part 1. Have students enter their scores on their **Fluency Graph.**

Selecting Books

The books in each set are leveled so students can start with any book in the set. However, students generally find contemporary fiction easier to read than nonfiction and retold classics.

On pages 10–11 you will find **Book Summaries** that give a brief outline of each book.

- If the book is a retold classic, information about the original author is included.
- If the book is a good tool for teaching a literary term, the term is explained. The teacher should teach the term before the students begin reading.
- The last section includes other resources—books, films, or Web sites—that contain related information. These resources can be used for extra credit, reports, projects, and so on. Evaluate all books, films, and Web sites to confirm appropriateness of the content prior to sharing these materials with students.

Express Yourself

Using *Ravenscourt* Books

Introducing the Series

1. Write the series theme on the board.
   - Tell the students that the books in the set all relate in some way to this common theme.
   - Brainstorm ideas about the theme, and write the students' ideas on a large sheet of chart paper. Include words, topics, and types of stories related to the theme. Post this list for student reference.
2. The books in each set represent several genres—fiction, nonfiction, biography, science fiction, historical fiction, retold classics, and so on.
   - Ask the students to read the title and the summary on the back of the book they chose.
   - Have the students predict how their book relates to the theme.
   - If the book is nonfiction, ask the student to predict what kinds of questions it could answer.

Whole-Class Instruction

The following sections are designed for whole-class instruction but may be modified for small groups or individual instruction.

Set up classes in the *Evaluation and Tracking Software,* or make a copy of the **Individual Progress Chart** for each student.

Assessing Fluency

Make a class set of copies of the **Fluency Graph** on page 9 of the *Teacher's Guide.* Follow these steps to **ASSESS STUDENTS' INITIAL ORAL-READING FLUENCY.**

1. Have the student read a passage that is set at the appropriate length (60–150 words) and at the appropriate instructional reading level (at least 95 percent accuracy).
   - The **Fluency Passage** section can be found after the **Thinking and Writing** section for each book.
2. Ask the student to do a one-minute reading of the unrehearsed passage.
3. Ask the student whether she or he is ready.
   - Then say: **Please begin.**
4. Follow along as the student reads.
   - When an error occurs, mark the error.
   - Count the following as errors: mispronunciations, omissions, substitutions, insertions, and failure to identify a word within three seconds.
   - Don't mark words the student self-corrects.
   - Don't mark off for proper nouns.
5. At the end of one minute, make a vertical line on the page after the last word read.
6. Count the number of words up to the last word read.
7. Subtract the number of errors to determine the wcpm.
8. Enter the number of words read correctly on the student's **Fluency Graph** by filling in the column to the appropriate number.
9. At the bottom of the graph, circle the number of errors made.
10. Review any words the student missed and provide practice on those words. The minimum goals for fluency are the following:
    - The goal for students who have completed *Decoding A* or have equivalent skills is to read the books in **Getting Started** at a minimum rate of 60 wcpm.
    - The goal for students who have completed *Comprehension A* or have equivalent skills is to read the books in **Discovery** at a minimum rate of 60 wcpm.
    - The goal for students who have completed *Decoding B1* or have equivalent skills is to read the books in **Anything's Possible** at a minimum rate of 90 wcpm.
    - The goal for students who have completed *Comprehension B1* or have equivalent skills is to read the books in **The Unexpected** at a minimum rate of 90 wcpm.

Express Yourself

Using *Ravenscourt* Books

- The goal for students who have completed *Decoding B2* or have equivalent skills is to read the books in **Express Yourself** at a minimum rate of 130 wcpm.
- The goal for students who have completed *Comprehension B2* or have equivalent skills is to read the books in **Overcoming Adversity** at a minimum rate of 130 wcpm.
- The goal for students who have completed Lesson 60 of *Decoding C* or have equivalent skills is to read the books in **Moving Forward** at a minimum rate of 150 wcpm.
- The goal for students who have completed Lesson 60 of *Comprehension C* or have equivalent skills is to read the books in **Reaching Goals** at a minimum rate of 150 wcpm.

Word Lists

Follow this procedure to preteach the words for each chapter of every book.

1. Provide students with a copy of the **Word Lists** page, or copy the words onto the board. Underline word parts if appropriate.
2. Begin with *Proper Nouns* by saying:
   - **These are the names of important people and places in Chapter 1.**
   - **Touch the first word in the column.**
   - Point to an underlined word part (if necessary) and say: **What sound?** (Signal.)
   - **What word?** (Signal.)
   - (Repeat until firm.)
3. For difficult and irregular words, say:
   - **Touch the word.**
   - **The word is _____.** (Signal.)
   - **What word?** (Signal.)
   - **Spell _____.** (Signal for each letter.)
   - **What word?** (Signal.)
   - (Repeat until firm.)
4. Follow the same procedure with *Unfamiliar Words*. Discuss the meanings of the words. Use the words in sentences as needed. The *Word Meanings* category is comprised of the words used in the *Word Meanings* section of **Building Background,** so some of the words may be familiar. Only use the following procedure for unfamiliar words.
   - Point to each unfamiliar word, say the word, and then say **What does _____ mean?** (Call on individual students.)
   - (Repeat until firm.)

Building Background

Use the **Building Background** section in the *Teacher's Guide* or on the *Evaluation and Tracking Software.* You can use this section as a whole-class activity or as an independent activity.

Whole-Class Activity

1. Divide the students into small groups. Hand out copies of the **Building Background** page for that book.
2. Read the questions in the *What You Know* section. Have the groups discuss the questions and write an answer for them. Have a member of each group read the group's answers to the class.
3. Read the words in the *Word Meanings* section.
   - Then read the directions and go over each question with the students and say, **Which word best answers this question?** (Call on individual students.)
   - Repeat this procedure for all of the words. (Note: If the directions indicate that the questions should be answered once the words have been introduced in the book, go over each word again after the students have read the word in context and have them answer the question associated with that word.)
4. Collect the papers and score them based on the number of correct answers. Refer to the **Answer Key** for each book.

Using Ravenscourt Books

Independent Activity

1. Hand out copies of the **Building Background** page. Have students take turns reading each question in the *What You Know* section. Have students write their answers before proceeding to the next question.
2. Have students read the words in the *Word Meanings* section. Then have them read the directions and complete the section.
   - When students are finished, collect the papers and score them based on completion and effort. Refer to the **Answer Key** for each book.

The teacher may enter the scores on the **Individual Progress Chart** found in the *Teacher's Guide* or on the *Evaluation and Tracking Software.*

Reading the Chapter

First, the students listen to a fluent reader read the chapter. The fluency model may be the teacher, a parent, a tutor, a teacher's aide, a peer, or the *Fluency Audio CDs.* Students read along, tracking the text with their fingers. Next, students take turns reading the chapter with their peer partner. An individual student reads aloud to the teacher, tutor, or parent, who gives feedback, points out missed words, and models, using punctuation, to improve expressive reading.

Chapter Quiz

After the second reading of the chapter, the student takes the **Chapter Quiz**. The quizzes have multiple-choice, true-or-false, sequence, and short-answer questions. The chapter quizzes are available on the *Evaluation and Tracking Software* or as blackline masters in the *Teacher's Guide.* Use the **Answer Keys** to score the blackline masters and enter scores on the **Individual Progress Chart** found on page 8. The *Evaluation and Tracking Software* will automatically grade and record the scores for all non-short-answer questions for each **Chapter Quiz.**

Students should take each quiz once and do their best the first time. Students must score a minimum of 80 percent to continue. If the student does not score 80 percent, he or she should reread the chapter before retaking the quiz.

Fluency Practice

Fluency practice improves comprehension. The teacher may choose different ways to practice fluency, depending on the student's needs. For students who are close to the target rate, have the student reread the whole chapter using one of these techniques:

- **Echo reading** A fluent reader reads a sentence aloud, and the student *echoes* it—repeats it with the same intonation and phrasing.
- **Unison or choral reading** A pair, group, or class reads a chapter aloud together.
- **Paired reading** The student reads a page aloud and receives feedback from his or her peer partner. Record the fluency scores on the **Fluency Graph** found in the *Teacher's Guide* or on the *Evaluation and Tracking Software.* Recording progress motivates student achievement.

For students who are significantly below the target rate, conduct **REPEATED READINGS TO IMPROVE ORAL-READING FLUENCY.** The student will reread the passages marked by asterisks in each of the books' chapters.

1. Set a target rate for the passage.
   - The target rate should be high enough to require the student to reread the passage several times.
   - A reasonable target rate is 40 percent higher than the baseline level.
   - For example, if the student initially reads the passage at a rate of 60 wcpm, the target rate for that passage would be 84 wcpm (**60** x .40 = 24; **60** + 24 = 84).

Using Ravenscourt Books

2. Have the student listen to the passage read fluently by a skilled reader or on the corresponding *Fluency Audio CD* while following along, pointing to the words as they are read.
3. After listening to the fluency model, have the student reread the same passage aloud for one minute.
   - A partner listens and records errors but does not interrupt the reader during the one-minute timed reading.
   - If the student makes more than six errors, he or she should listen to the fluency model again.
4. The student should read the same passage three to five times during the session or until the target rate is met, whichever comes first.
   - After each rereading, the student records the wcpm on his or her **Fluency Graph.**
   - If the target rate is not met, have the student read the same passage again the next day.
   - If the target rate is met, the student repeats the procedure with the next chapter.

Thinking and Writing

Many state assessments require students to produce extended writing about a story or an article they have read. Like **Building Background,** this section is not computer-scored and may be used in one of several ways. The *Think About It* section is intended to help students summarize what they have read and to relate the book to other books in the set, to the theme, or to the students' life experiences.

1. The questions in the *Think About It* section can be used for discussion.
   - Students discuss the questions in small groups and then write their individual responses on the blackline masters or using the *Evaluation and Tracking Software.*
   - The teacher may score the response using a variety of rubrics. For example, the teacher could give points for all reasonable responses in complete sentences that begin with a capital letter and end with appropriate punctuation.
2. For certain students, the teacher may ask the questions and prompt the student to give a thoughtful oral response.
3. Another option is to use *Think About It* as a mini-assessment. Have the students answer the questions independently on paper or using the *Evaluation and Tracking Software.*

The *Write About It* section gives students extended practice writing about what they have read. Students may write for as long as time allows.

The students may answer on the blackline master or use the *Evaluation and Tracking Software.* To motivate students, the *Evaluation and Tracking Software* includes a spelling checker and a variety of fonts and colors for students to choose from. This section is teacher-scored. Scores may be entered on a copy of the **Individual Progress Chart** or on the *Evaluation and Tracking Software.*

Students may keep their essays in a writing portfolio. At the end of the term students choose one of their essays to improve using the writing process. The final question in each *Write About It* section asks students to complete one of the graphic organizers that can be found as blackline masters in the back of this *Teacher's Guide* or on the *Evaluation and Tracking Software.* Graphic organizers are a structured, alternative writing experience. There are Book Report Forms, a What I Know/What I Learned Chart, a Sequencing Chart, and so on. Scores may be entered on the blackline master or *Evaluation and Tracking Software* version of the **Individual Progress Chart.**

Express Yourself

Individual Progress Chart

- Enter the percentage correct score for each quiz or activity.

Name: _____ Class: _____

Book Title	Building Background	Chapter 1 Quiz	Chapter 2 Quiz	Chapter 3 Quiz	Chapter 4 Quiz	Chapter 5 Quiz	Chapter 6 Quiz	Thinking and Writing	Graphic Organizer
Thousand-Mile Words									
They Landed One Night									
Bidding on the Past									
Blues King: The Story of B. B. King									
Sports Superstars									
Art for All!									
The Last Leaf and The Gift									
Oliver Twist									

Express Yourself

Fluency Graph

Name: _____ Class: _____

WCPM RATE
Number of words read correctly in one minute

1. Read a fluency passage for one minute. 2. Find the next open column. 3. Color the column to the number that shows how far you read. 4. Mark the number of errors in the chart at the bottom.

ERRORS — Above 6

Express Yourself

9

Book Summaries

Thousand-Mile Words
By Hilary Mac Austin

Summary
After Tino's father goes back to Japan, Tino finds it difficult to speak. This causes problems in his new school. At home, Tino's mother arranges for Tino to start e-mailing his cousin in Japan, Taku. The two exchange *haikus*—a form of Japanese poetry. Soon, Tino begins speaking in haikus to help him at school. Then Taku writes a haiku about his father, upsetting Tino, who misses his own dad. But, with encouragement from his mother, Tino is able to resume his e-mail exchange with Taku and starts an e-mail to his father.

Literary Terms
Fiction: a piece of literature that is invented

Coming-of-Age Story: main character is initiated into adulthood through knowledge, experience, or both; changes may be from ignorance to knowledge, innocence to experience, false view of the world to correct view, idealism to realism, or immature responses to mature responses

Other Resources
Book: Marshall, James. *Someone is Talking About Hortense* (Houghton Mifflin, 2000)

Movie: *The Parent Trap* (1998)

Web site: http://www.thebeehive.org/Templates/Family/Level3Image.aspx?PageId=1.528.734.736

They Landed One Night
By Jennifer Weinstein

Summary
In October 1938, the Rivera family purchases a new radio. After arranging a radio nook in the basement, friends of the Rivera brothers are invited for an evening of listening. The boys hear that a nearby farm is being invaded by aliens from Mars. They call their parents downstairs to listen to the reports. When their parents are convinced by the reporter, they drive the friends home and consider leaving town. As they make their decision, the radio announcer says they have actually been listening to *The War of the Worlds* by H. G. Wells.

Literary Terms
Science Fiction: an adventure story often set in other times or on other planets; often includes advanced technology, spaceships, robots, or aliens

Suspense: arousing the reader's curiosity or making the reader wonder what will happen next

Setting: the story environment; its time and place

Other Resources
Book: Costain Collins, Paul And Meredith. *Lost in Space (Thrillogy; 3 Science Fiction Stories)* (Sundance Publications, Limited, 2000)

Movie: *Lost in Space (New Line Platinum Series)* (1998)

Web site: http://www.kids.gov/k_space.htm

Bidding on the Past
By Jennifer Weinstein

Summary
Although Regine thinks her grandfather's favorite types of music—jazz and blues—are boring, she accompanies him to an auction of jazz and blues memorabilia. As the day progresses, Regine begins to appreciate these musical styles. Her grandfather is partly responsible for this. He tells her about the lives of several great jazz and blues singers and musicians, including Louis Armstrong, Ella Fitzgerald, Buddy Rich, and Robert Johnson. She discovers the historical roots of jazz and blues and discovers the impact each had on the music she likes. She finally realizes that these musical styles transcend age, race, and culture.

Literary Terms
Dialogue: the words spoken by characters in a story

Flashback: a past event that is told out of order

Other Resources
Books: Daly, Niki. *Ruby Sings the Blues* (Bloomsbury USA Children's Books, 2005); Nolan, Han. *Born Blue* (Harcourt Paperbacks; Reprint edition, 2003)

Movie: *St. Louis Blues* (2006)

Web sites: http://42explore.com/jazz.htm
http://www.history-of-rock.com/blues.htm

Blues King: The Story of B. B. King
By C. L. Collins

Summary
Although today he is one of the most popular blues musicians in the world and one of the best blues guitarists alive, B. B. King had to work hard to gain that recognition. He was born Riley B. King, a poor boy who worked as a sharecropper, picking cotton alongside his grandmother in the Mississippi Delta. There he learned to play the guitar and express the pain of segregation and the life of a sharecropper through blues music. From those beginnings, King grew to be a popular musician, defining blues music and helping to keep it alive throughout his long career.

Literary Term
Biography: an account of a person's life written by another person

Other Resources
Books: Adoff, Jaime. *Jimi & Me* (Jump At The Sun, 2007); Shirley, David. *Everyday I Sing the Blues: The Story of B.B. King (An Impact Biography)* (Franklin Watts, 1995)

Movies: *B.B. King Blues Session* (2005); *The Jazz Channel Presents B.B. King* (2001)

Web sites: http://www.bbking.com/default.asp
http://www.rockhall.com/hof/inductee.asp?id=137

Book Summaries

Sports Superstars
By Elizabeth Laskey

Summary
Many famous athletes found true success by overcoming social barriers. Swimmer Donna de Varona wanted to play baseball, but she was excluded because she was female. She turned to swimming, only to find the same prejudices. Oscar Robinson loved basketball, but his family was poor, and he played his first games with cans rather than a basketball. Billie Jean King fought against pay inequalities for women in sports, especially in tennis. These are a few of the stories of courage and endurance found in this chronicle of sports superstars.

Literary Term
Nonfiction: a factual piece of literature

Other Resources
Book: Nichols, Catherine. *Record Breakers: A Chapter Book (True Tales: Sports)* (Children's Press (CT), 2005)

Movies: *Like Mike* (2002); *The Sandlot* (1993)

Web site: http://www.libraryspot.com/biographies/athletes.htm

Art for All!
By Linda Barr

Summary
Not all art is found in museums. *Public art* is art in public places. In recent history, there have been many different types of public art. Mexican artist Diego Rivera's huge mural paintings helped start a mural movement. In South Africa, community murals on buildings show how society has changed. Christo and Jeanne-Claude Javacheff take years to plan their public art and display it for only a short time. Some other forms of public art discussed are the Vietnam Veterans Memorial, *Tilted Arc*, and ancient cave paintings.

Literary Term
Nonfiction: a factual piece of literature

Other Resources
Books: Dewey, Jennifer. *Stories on Stone: Rock Art: Images from the Ancient Ones* (University of New Mexico Press, 2003); Lapierre, Yvette and Lois Sloan. *Native American Rock Art: Messages from the Past* (Charlesbridge Publishing, 1994)

Movie: *How Art Made the World* (2006)

Web sites: http://www7.nationalgeographic.com/ngm/data/2001/08/01/html/ft_20010801.6.html
http://www.italianfrescoes.com/

The Last Leaf and The Gift
Retold by Nancy J. Nielsen

Summary
This book retells two O. Henry short stories. In "The Last Leaf," two young artists share an apartment in Greenwich Village. When one of them contracts pneumonia, she watches leaves drop from the vine outside her window, believing she will die when the last leaf falls. In "The Gift," Juan and Della, a young Puerto Rican couple, are celebrating their first anniversary. Love moves each to sell a prized possession to buy the perfect gift for the other.

Author
O. Henry was born William Sydney Porter in 1862. After fleeing the country to escape embezzlement charges, Porter returned to be with his sick wife. While in prison he began writing short stories. After his release he settled in New York City. He continued writing until his death in 1910.

Literary Terms
Setting: the story environment; its time and place

Plot: sequence of events with rising action, conflict, climax, and resolution

Irony: the difference between the expected results of a situation and the actual results

Other Resources
Book: Vande Velde, Vivian. *Three Good Deeds* (Harcourt Children's Books, 2005)

Movie: *Tuck Everlasting* (2002)

Web site: http://www.ci.austin.tx.us/parks/ohenry.htm

Oliver Twist
Retold by Kathleen Thompson

Summary
Oliver Twist was born in a workhouse and faced much hardship during his young life. Oliver ran away to London where he lived with a group of thieves led by a man named Fagin. After being wrongly accused of stealing, Oliver was taken in by Mr. Brownlow. But Oliver was returned to Fagin and forced to break into Mrs. Maylie's house. The mystery of Oliver's identity is unraveled when Mrs. Maylie decided to take care of Oliver.

Author
Charles Dickens (1812–1870) was one of the most influential novelists of the Victorian era. His novels, which include *A Tale of Two Cities*, *Great Expectations*, and *A Christmas Carol*, often dealt with the social and political conditions of England during the time.

Literary Terms
Plot: sequence of events with rising action, conflict, climax, and resolution

Foreshadowing: an author's hints about events that will occur later in the story

Other Resources
Books: Dahl, Roald. *Danny, the Champion of the World* (Puffin, 1998); Dahl, Roald. *Boy: Tales of Childhood* (Puffin; Reissue edition, 1999)

Movie: *Oliver Twist* (1985)

Web site: http://www.ac-nancy-metz.fr/enseign/anglais/Henry/OT.htm

Express Yourself

Building Background

Name _____ Date _____

Thousand-Mile Words
What You Know

Write answers to these questions.

1. What would it feel like to start at a new school where you didn't know anyone? _____
_____

2. Why do you think some people write poetry? _____
_____

3. Do you express yourself better when you speak or when you write? Why?
_____
_____

Word Meanings
Synonyms and Antonyms

Look for these words as you read your chapter book. When you find a word, write a synonym or antonym for the word.

Synonyms

fault: _____

usual: _____

weirdo: _____

Antonyms

beautiful: _____

nervous: _____

prey: _____

12　　　　　　　　　　　　　　　　　　　　　　Express Yourself • Book 1

Word Lists

Thousand-Mile Words

Unfamiliar Words	Word Meanings	Proper Nouns	
aloud, old-fashioned	weirdo	Valentino Ishiro	Chapter 1
cousin, haiku, poem, poetry, relief, reply, sputtered, syllables, written	nervous	Japanese, Taku, Uncle Hiroshi	Chapter 2
noticed	beautiful	Tanaka	Chapter 3
attitude, concentrate, example, mentioned, patience, relieved, worse	prey		Chapter 4
echoes, future, method	usual		Chapter 5
completed	fault		Chapter 6

Express Yourself • Book 1

13

Chapter Quiz

Name _____ Date _____

Thousand-Mile Words
Chapter 1, "Talk to Me"

Number the events in order from 1 to 5.

____ Tino sighs and stands up.

____ Mrs. Furman introduces Tino as Valentino Ishiro.

____ Mrs. Furman asks Tino to repeat himself.

____ Tino can't tell the class about his old school.

____ Tino wants to be invisible.

Number the events in order from 6 to 10.

____ Tino's mom says there is a surprise on the computer.

____ Tino hears the word *weirdo*, but nobody talks to him.

____ Mrs. Furman tells Tino she will be his homeroom and English teacher.

____ Tino's mom asks about his day.

____ Tino fears his new teachers will think he is stupid because he doesn't talk much.

Read the question, and write your answer.

What would you notice about Tino's looks? What would you notice about his personality? _____

_____

Chapter Quiz

Name _____ Date _____

Thousand-Mile Words
Chapter 2, "Taku's Haikus"

Mark each statement *T* for true or *F* for false.

____ 1. Tino and Taku are cousins.

____ 2. Taku is four years older than Tino.

____ 3. Tino's mom looks up the word *haiku*.

____ 4. Haiku is a kind of old American poetry.

____ 5. Haiku has four lines.

____ 6. Tino's first e-mail to Taku is not in haiku form.

____ 7. When it is four in the afternoon where Tino lives, it is seven in the morning on the next day in Kyoto.

____ 8. Tino's first haiku to Taku is simple.

____ 9. Taku sends a haiku to Tino saying he is going to bed.

____ 10. Tino writes a haiku to Taku about how much he likes school.

Read the question, and write your answer.

Why does Tino agree to write an e-mail to Taku? _____

_____

Express Yourself • Book 1

Chapter Quiz

Name _____ Date _____

Thousand-Mile Words
Chapter 3, "Haiku Moments"

Fill in the bubble beside the answer for each question.

1. Why does Tino like haikus?
   - Ⓐ They remind him of his dad in Japan.
   - Ⓑ They are about counting syllables, not about words.
   - Ⓒ They are simple, and they don't waste words.

2. Why does Tino start paying more attention to his teachers and classmates?
   - Ⓐ He is looking for "haiku moments."
   - Ⓑ He wants to find someone with whom he can be friends.
   - Ⓒ He does not want to seem stupid.

3. What is described in the haiku "My Day"?
   - Ⓐ Taku's school day
   - Ⓑ Tino's first day at the new school
   - Ⓒ Tino's fears about not being able to talk aloud

4. To what animal does Tino compare Mrs. Furman?
   - Ⓐ a crane
   - Ⓑ an owl
   - Ⓒ a fish

Read the question, and write your answer.

Why do you think it becomes easier and easier for Tino to write haikus?

_____

_____

Express Yourself • Book 1

Chapter Quiz

Name _____ Date _____

Thousand-Mile Words
Chapter 4, "Tied in Knots"

Number the events in order from 1 to 5.

____ Tino worries that the school might call his mom.

____ Mrs. Furman asks to see Tino after school.

____ Tino's teachers begin to complain about his attitude.

____ Taku's haiku gives Tino the idea to use a type of haiku to help him talk in school.

____ Taku writes he is worried about a big test.

Mark each statement *T* for true or *F* for false.

____ 1. Mr. Solomon calls on Tino.

____ 2. Tino gives his answer in a loud voice.

____ 3. Mr. Solomon does not like Tino's answer.

____ 4. Tino is relieved and happy about his haiku-like answer.

Read the question, and write your answer.

Why do Tino's teachers complain about his attitude? _____

_____

_____

Express Yourself • Book 1

Chapter Quiz

Name _____ Date _____

Thousand-Mile Words
Chapter 5, "Echoes"

Fill in the bubble beside the answer for each question.

1. How does Tino's "haiku method" help him?
   - Ⓐ It helps him answer questions aloud in class.
   - Ⓑ It helps him write better poems to Taku.
   - Ⓒ It helps make him very popular in school.

2. Why does Tino like Friday afternoons?
   - Ⓐ There is no school the next day.
   - Ⓑ He and Taku can e-mail for a long time.
   - Ⓒ Tino's mom waits for him at home.

3. What does Tino write in the haiku about his mother?
   - Ⓐ She worries about Tino's future.
   - Ⓑ She wants Tino to talk more.
   - Ⓒ She tugs words from her book.

4. Why did Tino's dad leave Tino and his mom?
   - Ⓐ He was mad at them.
   - Ⓑ He missed Japan, so he went back.
   - Ⓒ He needed a job.

Read the question, and write your answer.

Why is Taku worried about Tino at the end of this chapter?

_____

_____

Express Yourself • Book 1

Chapter Quiz

Name _____ Date _____

Thousand-Mile Words
Chapter 6, "Stepping Word to Word"

Mark each statement *T* for true or *F* for false.

___ 1. Tino writes a haiku to explain why he left his computer.

___ 2. Taku apologizes to Tino in a formal haiku.

___ 3. Tino asks if Taku knows Tino's father in Japan.

___ 4. Taku claims he knows Tino's dad well.

___ 5. Tino's father is happy in Japan.

___ 6. Tino's mom says she should have talked to Tino about his dad.

___ 7. Tino's mom does not miss Tino's dad.

___ 8. Tino's mom does not want Tino to write to his dad.

___ 9. Tino says he will not try to write to his dad.

___ 10. The last haiku of the story is like old haikus because it has five lines that were written by two people.

Read the question, and write your answer.

Why do you think Tino's father is silent? _____

_____

_____

Express Yourself • Book 1 19

Thinking and Writing

Name _____ Date _____

Thousand-Mile Words
Think About It

Write about or give an oral presentation for each question.

1. Why was it hard for Tino to talk aloud? _____
   _____
   _____

2. Tino learned that haikus use words to show one moment in time. If you could capture one moment in time, what moment would that be? Try to write a simple haiku about it. _____
   _____

3. Some people think a good poem shouldn't mean anything, but that it should simply "be." Why is this a good definition for a haiku?
   _____
   _____

4. Do you think Tino and his father will be able to talk with one another and get along through e-mail? Why or why not?
   _____

Write About It

Choose one of the questions below. Write your answer on a sheet of paper.

1. Pretend a new boy or girl has come to your school. He or she is very shy and is having a hard time fitting in. Write a list of things you can do to help the new student. Use complete sentences.

2. At the end of this story, Tino agrees to e-mail his father. Write the haiku you think Tino would write.

3. Complete the Cause and Effect Chart for this book.

Fluency Passages

Thousand-Mile Words

Chapter 1 *pages 4 and 5*

*"When will she stop?" he thought.	6
Finally she did.	9
"Well, thank you for letting us know that you like to be called Tino,"	23
Mrs. Furman said. "I want to welcome you to Woodhaven Middle School.	35
I am your homeroom teacher, and I am also your English teacher. I look	49
forward to seeing you in class. I am sure you'll do well here."	62
"Yeah," Tino mumbled as he sat back down.	70
Mrs. Furman gave Tino a sharp look, but she didn't say anything. For	83
the rest of homeroom she left Tino alone.	91
Tino was called on in every class that first day. He knew most of the	106
answers, and if the answers were only one word, he was okay. But if they	121
were more than one word, he couldn't answer. He* just shrugged. Some	133
teachers gave him sharp looks. Some sighed and shook their heads.	144

Chapter 6 *page 42*

*Tino read the e-mail again and again. He had always imagined his	12
father was happy in Japan. Tino imagined his father was relieved to be	25
away from him and his mom. He imagined his father laughed and spent	38
time with Taku and the rest of the family in Japan. But Tino's dad was not	54
just silent with Tino and his mom. He didn't talk to *anyone*. He was hiding.	69
He was ashamed.	72
"Mom," Tino called softly. "Look."	77
Tino's mom came over and read the e-mail.	85
"Your uncle never speaks of him," she whispered. "I thought he was	97
being kind by not bringing up your dad. I'm so sorry."	108
"You're sorry? Why?" Tino asked in surprise.	115
"Because I should have talked to you. But I was hiding, too, I guess. I*	130
didn't want to think about your dad."	137

- The target rate for **Express Yourself** is 130 wcpm. The asterisks (*) mark 130 words.
- Listen to the student read the passage. Count the number of words read in one minute and the number of errors.
- For the reading rate, subtract the number of errors from the total number of words read.
- Have students enter their scores on their **Fluency Graph.** See page 9.

Express Yourself • Book 1

Answer Key

Building Background

Name _____ Date _____

Thousand-Mile Words
What You Know
Write answers to these questions.

1. What would it feel like to start at a new school where you didn't know anyone? **Accept reasonable responses.**

2. Why do you think some people write poetry? **Ideas: because it is beautiful or fun; sometimes it is the best way to express feelings**

3. Do you express yourself better when you speak or when you write? Why? **Answers will vary.**

Word Meanings
Synonyms and Antonyms
Look for these words as you read your chapter book. When you find a word, write a synonym or antonym for the word.

Synonyms
fault: **responsibility, liability**
usual: **habitual, normal**
weirdo: **misfit**

Antonyms
beautiful: **ugly, unattractive**
nervous: **relaxed, calm**
prey: **predator, hunter**

Thousand-Mile Words

Chapter Quiz

Name _____ Date _____

Thousand-Mile Words
Chapter 1, "Talk to Me"
Number the events in order from 1 to 5.

- **4** Tino sighs and stands up.
- **2** Mrs. Furman introduces Tino as Valentino Ishiro.
- **3** Mrs. Furman asks Tino to repeat himself.
- **5** Tino can't tell the class about his old school.
- **1** Tino wants to be invisible.

Number the events in order from 6 to 10.

- **10** Tino's mom says there is a surprise on the computer.
- **8** Tino hears the word *weirdo*, but nobody talks to him.
- **6** Mrs. Furman tells Tino she will be his homeroom and English teacher.
- **9** Tino's mom asks about his day.
- **7** Tino fears his new teachers will think he is stupid because he doesn't talk much.

Read the question, and write your answer.

What would you notice about Tino's looks? What would you notice about his personality? **Tino is very tall. He is also shy.**

Thousand-Mile Words

Chapter Quiz

Name _____ Date _____

Thousand-Mile Words
Chapter 2, "Taku's Haikus"
Mark each statement *T* for true or *F* for false.

- **T** 1. Tino and Taku are cousins.
- **F** 2. Taku is four years older than Tino.
- **T** 3. Tino's mom looks up the word *haiku*.
- **F** 4. Haiku is a kind of old American poetry.
- **F** 5. Haiku has four lines.
- **T** 6. Tino's first e-mail to Taku is not in haiku form.
- **T** 7. When it is four in the afternoon where Tino lives, it is seven in the morning on the next day in Kyoto.
- **T** 8. Tino's first haiku to Taku is simple.
- **F** 9. Taku sends a haiku to Tino saying he is going to bed.
- **F** 10. Tino writes a haiku to Taku about how much he likes school.

Read the question, and write your answer.

Why does Tino agree to write an e-mail to Taku? **He knows his mom is happy about the e-mail idea, and he doesn't want to make his mom unhappy.**

Thousand-Mile Words

Chapter Quiz

Name _____ Date _____

Thousand-Mile Words
Chapter 3, "Haiku Moments"
Fill in the bubble beside the answer for each question.

1. Why does Tino like haikus?
   - Ⓐ They remind him of his dad in Japan.
   - Ⓑ They are about counting syllables, not about words.
   - ● They are simple, and they don't waste words.

2. Why does Tino start paying more attention to his teachers and classmates?
   - ● He is looking for "haiku moments."
   - Ⓑ He wants to find someone with whom he can be friends.
   - Ⓒ He does not want to seem stupid.

3. What is described in the haiku "My Day"?
   - ● Taku's school day
   - Ⓑ Tino's first day at the new school
   - Ⓒ Tino's fears about not being able to talk aloud

4. To what animal does Tino compare Mrs. Furman?
   - Ⓐ a crane
   - ● an owl
   - Ⓒ a fish

Read the question, and write your answer.

Why do you think it becomes easier and easier for Tino to write haikus? **Tino e-mails Taku new haikus every day after school. All the practice makes it easier and easier for Tino to write haikus.**

Thousand-Mile Words

Express Yourself • Book 1

Answer Key

Chapter Quiz

Name _____ Date _____

Thousand-Mile Words
Chapter 4, "Tied in Knots"

Number the events in order from 1 to 5.

__3__ Tino worries that the school might call his mom.
__2__ Mrs. Furman asks to see Tino after school.
__1__ Tino's teachers begin to complain about his attitude.
__5__ Taku's haiku gives Tino the idea to use a type of haiku to help him talk in school.
__4__ Taku writes he is worried about a big test.

Mark each statement T for true or F for false.

__T__ 1. Mr. Solomon calls on Tino.
__F__ 2. Tino gives his answer in a loud voice.
__F__ 3. Mr. Solomon does not like Tino's answer.
__T__ 4. Tino is relieved and happy about his haiku-like answer.

Read the question, and write your answer.

Why do Tino's teachers complain about his attitude? **Tino never participates in class. His teachers think he is being rude and disrespectful.**

Express Yourself • Book 1   17

Chapter Quiz

Name _____ Date _____

Thousand-Mile Words
Chapter 5, "Echoes"

Fill in the bubble beside the answer for each question.

1. How does Tino's "haiku method" help him?
   ● It helps him answer questions aloud in class.
   Ⓑ It helps him write better poems to Taku.
   Ⓒ It helps make him very popular in school.

2. Why does Tino like Friday afternoons?
   Ⓐ There is no school the next day.
   ● He and Taku can e-mail for a long time.
   Ⓒ Tino's mom waits for him at home.

3. What does Tino write in the haiku about his mother?
   Ⓐ She worries about Tino's future.
   Ⓑ She wants Tino to talk more.
   ● She tugs words from her book.

4. Why did Tino's dad leave Tino and his mom?
   Ⓐ He was mad at them.
   ● He missed Japan, so he went back.
   Ⓒ He needed a job.

Read the question, and write your answer.

Why is Taku worried about Tino at the end of this chapter? **Tino is not replying to the e-mails Taku sent.**

18   Express Yourself • Book 1

Chapter Quiz

Name _____ Date _____

Thousand-Mile Words
Chapter 6, "Stepping Word to Word"

Mark each statement T for true or F for false.

__T__ 1. Tino writes a haiku to explain why he left his computer.
__T__ 2. Taku apologizes to Tino in a formal haiku.
__T__ 3. Tino asks if Taku knows Tino's father in Japan.
__F__ 4. Taku claims he knows Tino's dad well.
__F__ 5. Tino's father is happy in Japan.
__T__ 6. Tino's mom says she should have talked to Tino about his dad.
__F__ 7. Tino's mom does not miss Tino's dad.
__F__ 8. Tino's mom does not want Tino to write to his dad.
__F__ 9. Tino says he will not try to write to his dad.
__T__ 10. The last haiku of the story is like old haikus because it has five lines that were written by two people.

Read the question, and write your answer.

Why do you think Tino's father is silent? **Ideas: lost in his own thoughts like Tino was; ashamed of leaving his family; misses his family**

Express Yourself • Book 1   19

Thinking and Writing

Name _____ Date _____

Thousand-Mile Words
Think About It

Write about or give an oral presentation for each question.

1. Why was it hard for Tino to talk aloud? **Ideas: was shy; was hurt and angry that his dad had left him and his mom to go to Japan; was upset that he couldn't speak**

2. Tino learned that haikus use words to show one moment in time. If you could capture one moment in time, what moment would that be? Try to write a simple haiku about it. **Answers will vary.**

3. Some people think a good poem shouldn't mean anything, but that it should simply "be." Why is this a good definition for a haiku? **Haikus try to show the world the way it is in one instant of time, like a photograph.**

4. Do you think Tino and his father will be able to talk with one another and get along through e-mail? Why or why not? **Accept reasonable responses.**

Write About It

Choose one of the questions below. Write your answer on a sheet of paper.

1. Pretend a new boy or girl has come to your school. He or she is very shy and is having a hard time fitting in. Write a list of things you can do to help the new student. Use complete sentences.

2. At the end of this story, Tino agrees to e-mail his father. Write the haiku you think Tino would write.

3. Complete the Cause and Effect Chart for this book.

20   Express Yourself • Book 1

Express Yourself • Book 1   23

Building Background

Name _____ Date _____

They Landed One Night
What You Know

Write answers to these questions.

1. Why was radio such an important invention? How did it change people's lives? _____
   _____

2. What is science fiction? _____
   _____

3. What would you do if you thought Earth was being invaded by space aliens? _____
   _____

4. Who was H. G. Wells? _____
   _____

Word Meanings
Matching

Look for these words as you read your chapter book. When you find a word, draw a line to connect the word with the correct definition.

alien	injury or harm that causes a loss
cozy	an expert in science
damage	a being from outer space
daydreaming	broad flat noodles baked with a sauce, usually of tomatoes, cheese, and meat or vegetables
lasagna	warm and comfortable
scientist	having pleasant, dreamy thoughts or wishes

Express Yourself • Book 2

Word Lists

They Landed One Night

Unfamiliar Words	Word Meanings	Proper Nouns	
bowls brightened electric equipment fuse	daydreaming	Angela Elisa New Jersey Robert Rivera Jr.	Chapter 1
dial exactly	cozy		Chapter 2
announcer comet explosions eyepiece interrupting meteoroid telescope	lasagna	Louis Armstrong New York City	Chapter 3
astronomer describing meteor object	alien		Chapter 4
continued creature tentacles	scientist		Chapter 5
neighbors scary shakily	damage	Kansas Ohio	Chapter 6

Express Yourself • Book 2

Chapter Quiz

Name _____ Date _____

They Landed One Night
Chapter 1, "Flickering Lights"

Mark each statement *T* for true or *F* for false.

_____ 1. Robbie lived in New York.

_____ 2. The Rivera family went to the beach every summer.

_____ 3. Robbie was dreaming of summer vacation when his sister awakened him.

_____ 4. Mrs. Rivera served cold chicken for dinner.

_____ 5. Robbie and Richie had played baseball in the morning.

_____ 6. The lights dimmed, became bright, and went back to normal.

_____ 7. The neighbor's porch light also dimmed and brightened.

_____ 8. Mr. Rivera called the electric company before finishing dinner.

_____ 9. The electric company claimed there was nothing wrong with their equipment.

_____ 10. The boys would wash the dishes while Mrs. Rivera relaxed.

Read the question, and write your answer.

What do you think caused the lights to dim and brighten?

_____

_____

_____

Chapter Quiz

Name _____ Date _____

They Landed One Night
Chapter 2, "A New Radio"

Number the events in order from 1 to 5.

____ Robbie could not get the radio to work.

____ Robbie and Richie cleaned the kitchen.

____ Elisa told Robbie the family was going to buy a new radio.

____ The children and Mr. Rivera worked in the basement.

____ The Rivera family went to the department store after breakfast.

Number the events in order from 6 to 10.

____ Robbie and Richie walked down the street to the Plants' home.

____ The Plant boys were given permission to go with Robbie and Richie.

____ All four boys went into the warm kitchen of the Riveras' home.

____ Mrs. Plant invited Robbie and Richie into the house.

____ Mr. and Mrs. Rivera agreed the boys could invite friends to come over after dinner.

Read the question, and write your answer.

Where did Mrs. Rivera want to put the new radio? Why?

_____

_____

_____

Express Yourself • Book 2

Chapter Quiz

Name _____ Date _____

They Landed One Night
Chapter 3, "Breaking News"

Fill in the bubble beside the answer for each question.

1. Why did the boys have to keep quiet in the basement?
   - Ⓐ Elisa was going to bed.
   - Ⓑ It was a school night.
   - Ⓒ Mr. and Mrs. Rivera did not want to be disturbed.

2. What was the first radio program the boys heard?
   - Ⓐ a news report
   - Ⓑ big band music
   - Ⓒ the weather report

3. Why did the boys leave the basement?
   - Ⓐ to find a telescope
   - Ⓑ to tell Mrs. Rivera what they had heard
   - Ⓒ to get some popcorn

4. What did the boys see with the telescope?
   - Ⓐ Mars
   - Ⓑ clouds and a bright light
   - Ⓒ meteors

Read the question, and write your answer.

Why did the boys borrow Mr. Rivera's telescope? _____

_____

_____

Chapter Quiz

Name _____ Date _____

They Landed One Night
Chapter 4, "A Meteor?"

Mark each statement *T* for true or *F* for false.

___ 1. The radio announcer was talking to an astronaut.

___ 2. The boys almost knocked Mrs. Rivera down the stairs.

___ 3. Richie saw a shooting star.

___ 4. Mrs. Rivera said the people on the radio were talking about Mars.

___ 5. The radio announcer reported a burning object had fallen in Grovers Mill, New Jersey.

___ 6. The reporter described something that looked just like a meteorite.

___ 7. The object was about 30 yards across and made of metal.

___ 8. Richie called his parents down to the basement.

___ 9. Mr. Rivera believed the boys.

___ 10. Robbie was afraid because he thought aliens had come from Mars to Earth.

Read the question, and write your answer.

What do you think will happen in the next chapter? _____

_____

_____

Express Yourself • Book 2

Chapter Quiz

Name _____ Date _____

They Landed One Night
Chapter 5, "Visitors from Mars"

Number the events in order from 1 to 5.

____ The top of the object opened.

____ The Riveras and their friends leaned closer to the radio and heard a faint scratching sound.

____ An alien came out of the spaceship.

____ The Riveras and the Plant boys stared silently at the radio.

____ The reporter asked the scientist if the object could be a meteorite.

Number the events in order from 6 to 10.

____ Mr. Rivera turned off the car radio.

____ The reporter claimed the creature had fired a "heat ray" into the sky.

____ Mr. Rivera did not allow Richie to turn off the radio.

____ Mr. Rivera decided to drive Billy and David home.

____ Mrs. Rivera brought Elisa downstairs to the basement.

Read the question, and write your answer.

Why do you think Mr. Rivera wanted Elisa to be in the basement?

_____

_____

_____

Chapter Quiz

Name _____ Date _____

They Landed One Night
Chapter 6, "The Attack?"

Fill in the bubble beside the answer for each question.

1. Where did Mrs. Green tell Mrs. Rivera she was going?
   - Ⓐ to her sister's house in Ohio
   - Ⓑ to Grovers Mill
   - Ⓒ to Billy and David's home

2. Why didn't the Riveras leave town right away?
   - Ⓐ They feared there might be alien ships everywhere.
   - Ⓑ The wind was too strong for them to drive safely, and it would take a long time to pack up their things.
   - Ⓒ Mr. Rivera did not believe the radio news.

3. What did Richie, Elisa, and Mrs. Rivera hear when they turned on the radio?
   - Ⓐ "Aliens are firing their heat rays at buildings!"
   - Ⓑ "Citizens of New Jersey, stay in your homes."
   - Ⓒ "We have just brought you *The War of the Worlds* by H. G. Wells."

4. What did Mr. Rivera do after hearing that the alien invasion was just a Halloween story?
   - Ⓐ He decided to write the radio station a letter.
   - Ⓑ He called the police station to make sure he had heard and understood correctly.
   - Ⓒ He laughed at the good joke.

Read the question, and write your answer.

Why was Mrs. Rivera upset that the radio station had broadcast such a scary story? _____

Express Yourself • Book 2　　31

Thinking and Writing

Name _____ Date _____

They Landed One Night
Think About It

Write about or give an oral presentation for each question.

1. Science fiction stories often involve scientists or things scientists would study. Why is *The War of the Worlds* considered science fiction?

2. If aliens were to invade Earth today, how would people learn of the invasion?

3. Do you think the radio station should have warned its audience before broadcasting *The War of the Worlds?* Why or why not?

Write About It

Choose one of the questions below. Write your answer on a sheet of paper.

1. At the end of this story, Mrs. Rivera says she will write a letter to the radio station to complain about its broadcast of *The War of the Worlds*. Write that letter. Be sure to tell the station what happened in the Rivera family. Let the station know why you are upset.

2. Write a newspaper article describing what happened the night *The War of the Worlds* was broadcast. Use information from the chapters in your article.

3. Pretend you are an alien coming out of your spaceship. Describe Earth and the earthlings you see for a radio show on your home planet.

4. Complete the Genres Chart for this book.

Fluency Passages

They Landed One Night

Chapter 1 *page 2*

*Robbie looked out the window of the Riveras' little brick house. The	12
sky was gray and heavy with clouds. A cold wind shook leaves from the	26
trees. Robbie watched a woman and a little girl across the street trying to	40
walk against the wind. The little girl held tight to the woman's coat.	53
Robbie thought about the cool breeze in his hair as the wind blew off	67
the ocean. He thought about the warm sun on his face as he lay on the hot	84
sand. He thought about the taste of salt water as he swam in the deep blue	100
sea. And he thought about being bounced around as their rented boat went	113
over the waves. He could almost feel the boat bouncing and shaking.	125
Suddenly, Robbie jumped. He had* fallen asleep on the couch	135
daydreaming about the beach.	139

Chapter 3 *pages 16 and 17*

*Mrs. Rivera stopped the boys on their way to the basement. "It's	12
already eight o'clock," she said. "Elisa is going to bed. Make sure you	25
boys keep quiet."	28
"We will, Mrs. Rivera," David said. "Our mom wants us home by	40
nine o'clock, so we won't be here too long."	49
Mrs. Rivera smiled and went to help Elisa get her clothes ready for	62
school the next day. The four boys went downstairs.	71
"Wow," Billy said when he saw the fixed-up basement. "This is great!	83
You have a place to sit and listen to the radio without anyone interrupting	97
you."	98
"Yeah," Robbie answered. "It turned out nice. I think Mom and Dad	110
wanted to give Richie and me a place where we could hang out with our	125
friends. Let's try out the* radio."	131

- The target rate for **Express Yourself** is 130 wcpm. The asterisks (*) mark 130 words.
- Listen to the student read the passage. Count the number of words read in one minute and the number of errors.
- For the reading rate, subtract the number of errors from the total number of words read.
- Have students enter their scores on their **Fluency Graph.** See page 9.

Answer Key

Building Background

Name _____ Date _____

They Landed One Night
What You Know

Write answers to these questions.

1. Why was radio such an important invention? How did it change people's lives? **Accept reasonable responses**

2. What is science fiction? **Science-fiction stories are based on science or what the future might hold.**

3. What would you do if you thought Earth was being invaded by space aliens? **Answers will vary.**

4. Who was H. G. Wells? **a famous science-fiction writer**

Word Meanings
Matching

Look for these words as you read your chapter book. When you find a word, draw a line to connect the word with the correct definition.

- alien — a being from outer space
- cozy — warm and comfortable
- damage — injury or harm that causes a loss
- daydreaming — having pleasant, dreamy thoughts or wishes
- lasagna — broad flat noodles baked with a sauce, usually of tomatoes, cheese, and meat or vegetables
- scientist — an expert in science

24 Express Yourself • Book 2

They Landed One Night

Chapter Quiz

Name _____ Date _____

They Landed One Night
Chapter 1, "Flickering Lights"

Mark each statement *T* for true or *F* for false.

- F 1. Robbie lived in New York.
- T 2. The Rivera family went to the beach every summer.
- T 3. Robbie was dreaming of summer vacation when his sister awakened him.
- F 4. Mrs. Rivera served cold chicken for dinner.
- F 5. Robbie and Richie had played baseball in the morning.
- T 6. The lights dimmed, became bright, and went back to normal.
- T 7. The neighbor's porch light also dimmed and brightened.
- F 8. Mr. Rivera called the electric company before finishing dinner.
- T 9. The electric company claimed there was nothing wrong with their equipment.
- T 10. The boys would wash the dishes while Mrs. Rivera relaxed.

Read the question, and write your answer.

What do you think caused the lights to dim and brighten?
Accept reasonable responses.

26 Express Yourself • Book 2

They Landed One Night

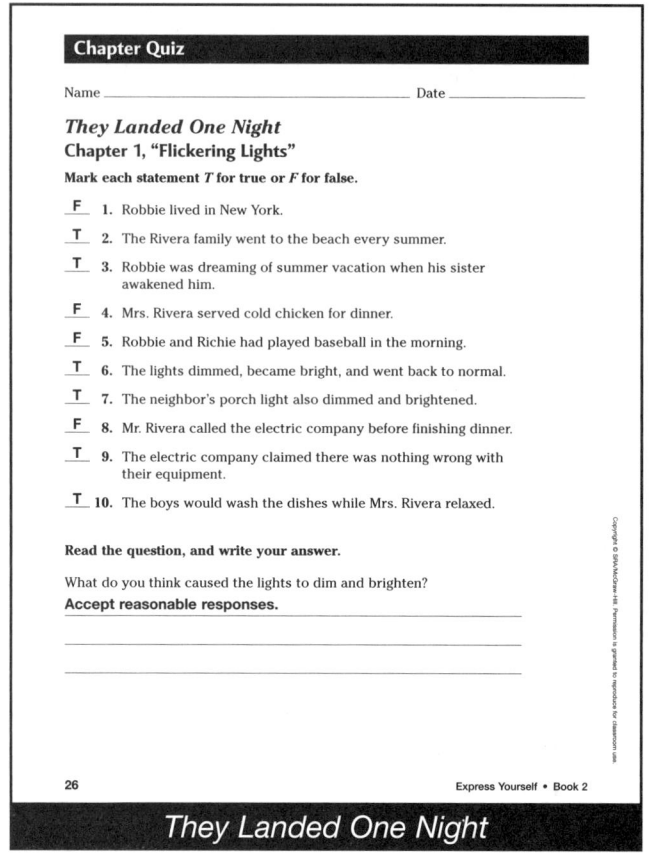

Chapter Quiz

Name _____ Date _____

They Landed One Night
Chapter 2, "A New Radio"

Number the events in order from 1 to 5.

- 2 Robbie could not get the radio to work.
- 1 Robbie and Richie cleaned the kitchen.
- 3 Elisa told Robbie the family was going to buy a new radio.
- 5 The children and Mr. Rivera worked in the basement.
- 4 The Rivera family went to the department store after breakfast.

Number the events in order from 6 to 10.

- 7 Robbie and Richie walked down the street to the Plants' home.
- 9 The Plant boys were given permission to go with Robbie and Richie.
- 10 All four boys went into the warm kitchen of the Riveras' home.
- 8 Mrs. Plant invited Robbie and Richie into the house.
- 6 Mr. and Mrs. Rivera agreed the boys could invite friends to come over after dinner.

Read the question, and write your answer.

Where did Mrs. Rivera want to put the new radio? Why?
in the basement; thought the basement would be nice little room for the children

Express Yourself • Book 2   27

They Landed One Night

Chapter Quiz

Name _____ Date _____

They Landed One Night
Chapter 3, "Breaking News"

Fill in the bubble beside the answer for each question.

1. Why did the boys have to keep quiet in the basement?
   - ● Elisa was going to bed.
   - Ⓑ It was a school night.
   - Ⓒ Mr. and Mrs. Rivera did not want to be disturbed.

2. What was the first radio program the boys heard?
   - Ⓐ a news report
   - Ⓑ big band music
   - ● the weather report

3. Why did the boys leave the basement?
   - ● to find a telescope
   - Ⓑ to tell Mrs. Rivera what they had heard
   - Ⓒ to get some popcorn

4. What did the boys see with the telescope?
   - Ⓐ Mars
   - ● clouds and a bright light
   - Ⓒ meteors

Read the question, and write your answer.

Why did the boys borrow Mr. Rivera's telescope? **The radio announcer said there had been explosions on Mars and that something now appeared to be moving quickly toward Earth. The boys wanted to see what it was.**

28 Express Yourself • Book 2

They Landed One Night

---

34   Express Yourself • Book 2

Answer Key

Chapter Quiz

Name _____ Date _____

They Landed One Night
Chapter 4, "A Meteor?"

Mark each statement *T* for true or *F* for false.

- **F** 1. The radio announcer was talking to an astronaut.
- **T** 2. The boys almost knocked Mrs. Rivera down the stairs.
- **F** 3. Richie saw a shooting star.
- **T** 4. Mrs. Rivera said the people on the radio were talking about Mars.
- **T** 5. The radio announcer reported a burning object had fallen in Grovers Mill, New Jersey.
- **F** 6. The reporter described something that looked just like a meteorite.
- **T** 7. The object was about 30 yards across and made of metal.
- **T** 8. Richie called his parents down to the basement.
- **F** 9. Mr. Rivera believed the boys.
- **T** 10. Robbie was afraid because he thought aliens had come from Mars to Earth.

Read the question, and write your answer.

What do you think will happen in the next chapter? **Answers will vary.**

Express Yourself • Book 2   29

They Landed One Night

Chapter Quiz

Name _____ Date _____

They Landed One Night
Chapter 5, "Visitors from Mars"

Number the events in order from 1 to 5.

- **4** The top of the object opened.
- **2** The Riveras and their friends leaned closer to the radio and heard a faint scratching sound.
- **5** An alien came out of the spaceship.
- **1** The Riveras and the Plant boys stared silently at the radio.
- **3** The reporter asked the scientist if the object could be a meteorite.

Number the events in order from 6 to 10.

- **9** Mr. Rivera turned off the car radio.
- **7** The reporter claimed the creature had fired a "heat ray" into the sky.
- **6** Mr. Rivera did not allow Richie to turn off the radio.
- **8** Mr. Rivera decided to drive Billy and David home.
- **10** Mrs. Rivera brought Elisa downstairs to the basement.

Read the question, and write your answer.

Why do you think Mr. Rivera wanted Elisa to be in the basement? **He thought the family would be safer together, and in the basement they could still get news from the radio.**

30   Express Yourself • Book 2

They Landed One Night

Chapter Quiz

Name _____ Date _____

They Landed One Night
Chapter 6, "The Attack?"

Fill in the bubble beside the answer for each question.

1. Where did Mrs. Green tell Mrs. Rivera she was going?
   - ● to her sister's house in Ohio
   - Ⓑ to Grovers Mill
   - Ⓒ to Billy and David's home

2. Why didn't the Riveras leave town right away?
   - ● They feared there might be alien ships everywhere.
   - Ⓑ The wind was too strong for them to drive safely, and it would take a long time to pack up their things.
   - Ⓒ Mr. Rivera did not believe the radio news.

3. What did Richie, Elisa, and Mrs. Rivera hear when they turned on the radio?
   - Ⓐ "Aliens are firing their heat rays at buildings!"
   - Ⓑ "Citizens of New Jersey, stay in your homes."
   - ● "We have just brought you *The War of the Worlds* by H. G. Wells."

4. What did Mr. Rivera do after hearing that the alien invasion was just a Halloween story?
   - Ⓐ He decided to write the radio station a letter.
   - ● He called the police station to make sure he had heard and understood correctly.
   - Ⓒ He laughed at the good joke.

Read the question, and write your answer.

Why was Mrs. Rivera upset that the radio station had broadcast such a scary story? **She and many others did not realize they had only been listening to a story, and they were very frightened.**

Express Yourself • Book 2   31

They Landed One Night

Thinking and Writing

Name _____ Date _____

They Landed One Night
Think About It

Write about or give an oral presentation for each question.

1. Science fiction stories often involve scientists or things scientists would study. Why is *The War of the Worlds* considered science fiction?
   Ideas: It involves science, astronomers, and space aliens; it deals with things that might be possible.

2. If aliens were to invade Earth today, how would people learn of the invasion? **from different news sources including television, online news, and radio**

3. Do you think the radio station should have warned its audience before broadcasting *The War of the Worlds*? Why or why not?
   Answers will vary.

Write About It

Choose one of the questions below. Write your answer on a sheet of paper.

1. At the end of this story, Mrs. Rivera says she will write a letter to the radio station to complain about its broadcast of *The War of the Worlds*. Write that letter. Be sure to tell the station what happened in the Rivera family. Let the station know why you are upset.

2. Write a newspaper article describing what happened the night *The War of the Worlds* was broadcast. Use information from the chapters in your article.

3. Pretend you are an alien coming out of your spaceship. Describe Earth and the earthlings you see for a radio show on your home planet.

4. Complete the Genres Chart for this book.

32   Express Yourself • Book 2

They Landed One Night

Express Yourself • Book 2   35

Building Background

Name _____ Date _____

Bidding on the Past
What You Know

Write answers to these questions.

1. Use a dictionary to define the following words: *jazz, blues, rock and roll,* and *folk music.* How are they connected to one another?

   _____

   _____

   _____

   _____

2. List at least six musical instruments. Circle the ones used by your favorite musical group. Put a square around those you think are used for jazz and blues. _____

3. What type of music do you enjoy most? Explain what it is and why you like it. _____

Word Meanings
Definitions

Look for these words as you read your chapter book. When you find one of these words, write its definition.

ballad: _____

cornet: _____

guitar: _____

influence: _____

pearl: _____

vaudeville: _____

36   Express Yourself • Book 3

Word Lists

Bidding on the Past

	Unfamiliar Words	Word Meanings	Proper Nouns
Chapter 1	admired auction education instruments jazz noticed raise serious	influence	John Coltrane Lincoln Center Jazz Orchestra Louis Armstrong Miles Davis Regine Wynton Marsalis
Chapter 2	improvisation improvise lobby microphone style	cornet	Satchmo New Orleans Mississippi River
Chapter 3	awards beautiful recordings scat songwriters syllables talent written	ballad	Apollo Theater Billie Holiday Ella Fitzgerald Frank Sinatra Harlem Ira Gershwin Nina Simone
Chapter 4	creative emotion interview melodies practiced tribute	vaudeville	Buddy Rich Gene Krupa
Chapter 5	practicing songwriting suit title	guitar	Keith Richards Robert Johnson
Chapter 6	businesswoman electronically entertainer guest popularity special	pearl	Benny Goodman Bessie Smith Gertrude "Ma" Rainey

Express Yourself • Book 3

Chapter Quiz

Name _____ Date _____

Bidding on the Past
Chapter 1, "Jazz Lives On"

Fill in the bubble beside the answer for each question.

1. Regine and her grandfather were driving to the city to
   - Ⓐ attend an auction.
   - Ⓑ attend a jazz festival.
   - Ⓒ visit a blues museum.

2. Grandpa Russell's favorite kinds of music are
   - Ⓐ blues and hip-hop.
   - Ⓑ rock and jazz.
   - Ⓒ jazz and blues.

3. John Coltrane experimented with new instruments like
   - Ⓐ saxophones.
   - Ⓑ African drums.
   - Ⓒ electric guitars.

4. Coltrane was
   - Ⓐ earnest.
   - Ⓑ serious about his art.
   - Ⓒ both A and B

Read the question, and write your answer.

Why does Regine's grandfather know so much about jazz and blues music?

_____

_____

Chapter Quiz

Name _____ Date _____

Bidding on the Past
Chapter 2, "Satchmo"

Mark each statement *T* for true or *F* for false.

_____ 1. People at the auction were mostly Grandpa Russell's age and older.

_____ 2. The auction included books, musical instruments, albums, and fancy dresses.

_____ 3. The jazz and blues items were auctioned together.

_____ 4. The family of Louis Armstrong gave a saxophone to the auction.

_____ 5. Armstrong learned to play cornet at a reform school when he was just 12 years old.

_____ 6. Armstrong played music on boats that went down the Mississippi River.

_____ 7. "Satchmo" was a nickname for Pops Foster.

_____ 8. Armstrong took jazz to other countries around the world.

_____ 9. Jazz music can be traced back to the time of slavery.

_____ 10. Improvisation is not used much in jazz.

Read the question, and write your answer.

How did Grandpa Russell link Armstrong to Regine's favorite kinds of music? _____

_____

_____

Express Yourself • Book 3

Chapter Quiz

Name _____ Date _____

Bidding on the Past
Chapter 3, "The First Lady of Song"

Mark each statement *T* for true or *F* for false.

____ 1. Ella Fitzgerald was the most popular female rock singer for over 50 years.

____ 2. Fitzgerald first began singing at the Apollo Theater in Harlem.

____ 3. Fitzgerald could make her voice sound like any instrument in the orchestra.

____ 4. Record companies wanted Fitzgerald to sing ballads.

____ 5. Many of Nina Simone's songs were about the civil rights movement.

____ 6. Billie Holiday's songs were about African American life.

____ 7. By singing song lyrics faster, Holiday gave jazz a style closer to blues.

____ 7. During her career, Fitzgerald recorded over 2,000 songs.

____ 9. Although she was a great singer, Fitzgerald never made it into the Grammy Hall of Fame.

____ 10. *Scat* is a type of singing that uses made-up words or syllables.

Read the question, and write your answer.

How did Fitzgerald help pave the way for female jazz singers?

_____

_____

_____

40   Express Yourself • Book 3

Chapter Quiz

Name _____ Date _____

Bidding on the Past
Chapter 4, "Traps the Drum Wonder"

Number the events in order from 1 to 5.

____ Buddy Rich played in some of the most popular bands in the country.

____ Rich started his own band.

____ Rich was a star in vaudeville shows.

____ Rich played for presidents, kings, and queens.

____ Today's great drummers made a CD tribute album to Rich.

Mark each statement *T* for true or *F* for false.

____ 1. Rich was a singer, drummer, and tap dancer in vaudeville.

____ 2. Rich practiced long and hard to be a good drummer.

____ 3. Rich tuned his drums to play melodies on them.

____ 4. When rock and roll took over, Rich's style no longer worked.

Read the question, and write your answer.

Why was Rich called *the* drummer? Give at least three reasons in your answer. _____

_____

_____

Express Yourself • Book 3   41

Chapter Quiz

Name _____ Date _____

Bidding on the Past
Chapter 5, "Father of Rock and Roll"

Fill in the bubble beside the answer for each question.

1. One item in the auction was Robert Johnson's
   - Ⓐ drums.
   - Ⓑ guitar.
   - Ⓒ music.

2. Which music styles can be traced to blues?
   - Ⓐ jazz and rock and roll
   - Ⓑ hip-hop and rap
   - Ⓒ both A and B

3. The birthplace of blues is
   - Ⓐ Mississippi.
   - Ⓑ Louisiana.
   - Ⓒ Alabama.

4. One of the things that made Johnson great was his
   - Ⓐ singing.
   - Ⓑ working relationship with W. C. Handy.
   - Ⓒ songwriting.

Read the question, and write your answer.

How can hip-hop and rap be traced back to slavery?

_____

_____

Chapter Quiz

Name _____ Date _____

Bidding on the Past
Chapter 6, "A Special Guest"

Number the events in order from 1 to 5.

____ Grandpa Russell wrote something on a piece of paper.

____ Regine and her grandfather left the blues auction.

____ On the way home, Regine listened to jazz music with new understanding and appreciation.

____ B. B. King was introduced to the audience.

____ Grandpa Russell and Regine looked at the silent auction items.

Mark each statement *T* for true or *F* for false.

____ 1. In the 1960s, Bessie Smith was the highest-paid African American entertainer in the country.

____ 2. The first electronically recorded album was *Cake Walking Babies*.

____ 3. Smith was the first woman to sing the blues.

____ 4. Grandpa Russell bid on an album signed by Coltrane.

Read the question, and write your answer.

What was the relationship between Smith and Gertrude "Ma" Rainey?

_____

_____

_____

Express Yourself • Book 3   43

Thinking and Writing

Name _____ Date _____

Bidding on the Past
Think About It

Write about or give an oral presentation for each question.

1. Compare your favorite kind of music with jazz and blues. In what ways are the three music styles similar? _____

2. How is improvisation like scat? How are they different?

   _____
   _____

3. Compare Armstrong with Fitzgerald. How did each of them change music and the culture around them? Which do you think had more impact? _____

4. Regine saw people of all races and ages at the auction. Why do you think jazz and blues appeal to such a wide variety of people?

   _____

Write About It

Choose one of the questions below. Write your answer on a sheet of paper.

1. Think about ways slavery shaped blues and jazz. How did blues and jazz impact the civil rights movement? Use your ideas to write a newspaper-style article about the important place music has in U.S. culture and history.

2. Based on this story, write a three-paragraph description of jazz and blues. Include a paragraph about the history of these two types of music. When you are done, listen to songs by three of the jazz and blues artists you read about in this book. Now write three new paragraphs describing jazz and blues. How did your understanding of the music change after hearing it?

3. Complete the Main Idea/Details Chart for this book.

Fluency Passages

Bidding on the Past

Chapter 2 *pages 8 and 9*

*The crowd grew quiet as a tall man stepped to the microphone.	12
"Good morning. We will begin the auction with items from the great jazz	25
musicians. After a break, we will look at items from the great blues artists.	39
Please remember that we are having this auction to help raise money for	52
music education in our schools.	57
"The first item up for bid was given to us by the family of the late	73
Louis Armstrong."	75
A pretty woman in a long blue dress brought out a shiny cornet.	88
"This cornet," the man told the crowd, "belonged to Armstrong. He	99
was also known as 'Satchmo.' He was born in New Orleans in 1901 and	113
died in 1971. The bidding will start at 10,000 dollars."	123
As people began shouting bids, Grandpa Russell* leaned over and	133
whispered in Regine's ear.	137

Chapter 4 *pages 26 and 27*

*"Krupa said he had been afraid to hear Rich play, because he had	13
heard Rich was so good.	18
"As I recall, Rich started playing drums when he was just a baby. His	32
mother and father were in vaudeville. Vaudeville shows had short acts like	44
comedy, singing, and dancing. It was a popular form of entertainment in	56
the early 1900s. They put Rich on stage when he was only 18 months old.	71
He was called 'Traps the Drum Wonder.'	78
"Even at that young age, Rich was a gifted drummer. He never had a	92
lesson and said he never practiced. He only played during shows. Somehow,	104
he just knew how to play.	110
"As a child, Rich was a star in many vaudeville shows. He was a pretty	125
good singer and tap dancer,* but drumming was where he made his mark.	138

- The target rate for **Express Yourself** is 130 wcpm. The asterisks (*) mark 130 words.
- Listen to the student read the passage. Count the number of words read in one minute and the number of errors.
- For the reading rate, subtract the number of errors from the total number of words read.
- Have students enter their scores on their **Fluency Graph.** See page 9.

Express Yourself • Book 3

Answer Key

Building Background

Name _____ Date _____

Bidding on the Past
What You Know
Write answers to these questions.

1. Use a dictionary to define the following words: *jazz, blues, rock and roll,* and *folk music*. How are they connected to one another?
   Jazz is music that started with Southern African Americans in the 19th century. Blues are sad, slow folk songs. Rock and roll developed from jazz and blues. Folk music is the music of the common people of a region.

2. List at least six musical instruments. Circle the ones used by your favorite musical group. Put a square around those you think are used for jazz and blues. **Answers will vary.**

3. What type of music do you enjoy most? Explain what it is and why you like it. **Accept reasonable responses.**

Word Meanings
Definitions
Look for these words as you read your chapter book. When you find one of these words, write its definition.

ballad: **a song or poem that tells a story in short verses**
cornet: **a musical instrument like the trumpet, but shorter**
guitar: **a musical instrument with six strings that is played by plucking the strings with the fingers or with a pick**
influence: **the power to act on or affect persons or things in ways that are either good or bad**
pearl: **a gem that is glossy, creamy white or blue-gray in color, and usually round in shape and is formed inside the shells of certain kinds of oysters**
vaudeville: **theatrical entertainment made up of a variety of songs, dances, and comic acts**

36 — Express Yourself • Book 3

Bidding on the Past

Chapter Quiz

Name _____ Date _____

Bidding on the Past
Chapter 1, "Jazz Lives On"
Fill in the bubble beside the answer for each question.

1. Regine and her grandfather were driving to the city to
   ● attend an auction.
   Ⓑ attend a jazz festival.
   Ⓒ visit a blues museum.

2. Grandpa Russell's favorite kinds of music are
   Ⓐ blues and hip-hop.
   Ⓑ rock and jazz.
   ● jazz and blues.

3. John Coltrane experimented with new instruments like
   Ⓐ saxophones.
   ● African drums.
   Ⓒ electric guitars.

4. Coltrane was
   Ⓐ earnest.
   Ⓑ serious about his art.
   ● both A and B

Read the question, and write your answer.

Why does Regine's grandfather know so much about jazz and blues music?
Ideas: his favorite kind of music; had played in a jazz band; studied jazz and blues and the people who made them famous

38 — Express Yourself • Book 3

Bidding on the Past

Chapter Quiz

Name _____ Date _____

Bidding on the Past
Chapter 2, "Satchmo"
Mark each statement *T* for true or *F* for false.

__F__ 1. People at the auction were mostly Grandpa Russell's age and older.
__T__ 2. The auction included books, musical instruments, albums, and fancy dresses.
__F__ 3. The jazz and blues items were auctioned together.
__F__ 4. The family of Louis Armstrong gave a saxophone to the auction.
__T__ 5. Armstrong learned to play cornet at a reform school when he was just 12 years old.
__T__ 6. Armstrong played music on boats that went down the Mississippi River.
__F__ 7. "Satchmo" was a nickname for Pops Foster.
__T__ 8. Armstrong took jazz to other countries around the world.
__T__ 9. Jazz music can be traced back to the time of slavery.
__F__ 10. Improvisation is not used much in jazz.

Read the question, and write your answer.

How did Grandpa Russell link Armstrong to Regine's favorite kinds of music? **Ideas: told her that Armstrong used lots of improvisation and that artists still copy the way he played; suggested that some of the bands she listens to use Armstrong's style**

Express Yourself • Book 3 — 39

Bidding on the Past

Chapter Quiz

Name _____ Date _____

Bidding on the Past
Chapter 3, "The First Lady of Song"
Mark each statement *T* for true or *F* for false.

__F__ 1. Ella Fitzgerald was the most popular female rock singer for over 50 years.
__T__ 2. Fitzgerald first began singing at the Apollo Theater in Harlem.
__T__ 3. Fitzgerald could make her voice sound like any instrument in the orchestra.
__F__ 4. Record companies wanted Fitzgerald to sing ballads.
__T__ 5. Many of Nina Simone's songs were about the civil rights movement.
__T__ 6. Billie Holiday's songs were about African American life.
__F__ 7. By singing song lyrics faster, Holiday gave jazz a style closer to blues.
__T__ 7. During her career, Fitzgerald recorded over 2,000 songs.
__F__ 9. Although she was a great singer, Fitzgerald never made it into the Grammy Hall of Fame.
__T__ 10. *Scat* is a type of singing that uses made-up words or syllables.

Read the question, and write your answer.

How did Fitzgerald help pave the way for female jazz singers?
Ideas: People liked her music; she was a great singer and improviser; she sang ballads, which helped other female singers tell stories through their own songs.

40 — Express Yourself • Book 3

Bidding on the Past

---

46 — Express Yourself • Book 3

Answer Key

Chapter Quiz

Name _____ Date _____

Bidding on the Past
Chapter 4, "Traps the Drum Wonder"

Number the events in order from 1 to 5.

_2_ Buddy Rich played in some of the most popular bands in the country.

_3_ Rich started his own band.

_1_ Rich was a star in vaudeville shows.

_4_ Rich played for presidents, kings, and queens.

_5_ Today's great drummers made a CD tribute album to Rich.

Mark each statement *T* for true or *F* for false.

_T_ 1. Rich was a singer, drummer, and tap dancer in vaudeville.

_F_ 2. Rich practiced long and hard to be a good drummer.

_T_ 3. Rich tuned his drums to play melodies on them.

_F_ 4. When rock and roll took over, Rich's style no longer worked.

Read the question, and write your answer.

Why was Rich called *the* drummer? Give at least three reasons in your answer. **Ideas: knew how to play drums; played fast, loud and hard; tuned his drums to play melodies; his style worked well for rock and roll**

Express Yourself • Book 3   41

Bidding on the Past

Chapter Quiz

Name _____ Date _____

Bidding on the Past
Chapter 5, "Father of Rock and Roll"

Fill in the bubble beside the answer for each question.

1. One item in the auction was Robert Johnson's
   - Ⓐ drums.
   - ● guitar.
   - Ⓒ music.

2. Which music styles can be traced to blues?
   - Ⓐ jazz and rock and roll
   - Ⓑ hip-hop and rap
   - ● both A and B

3. The birthplace of blues is
   - ● Mississippi.
   - Ⓑ Louisiana.
   - Ⓒ Alabama.

4. One of the things that made Johnson great was his
   - Ⓐ singing.
   - Ⓑ working relationship with W. C. Handy.
   - ● songwriting.

Read the question, and write your answer.

How can hip-hop and rap be traced back to slavery? **Blues developed as a way of life in slavery and a musical style after slavery. Hip-hop and rap both came from blues.**

42   Express Yourself • Book 3

Bidding on the Past

Chapter Quiz

Name _____ Date _____

Bidding on the Past
Chapter 6, "A Special Guest"

Number the events in order from 1 to 5.

_4_ Grandpa Russell wrote something on a piece of paper.

_2_ Regine and her grandfather left the blues auction.

_5_ On the way home, Regine listened to jazz music with new understanding and appreciation.

_1_ B. B. King was introduced to the audience.

_3_ Grandpa Russell and Regine looked at the silent auction items.

Mark each statement *T* for true or *F* for false.

_F_ 1. In the 1960s, Bessie Smith was the highest-paid African American entertainer in the country.

_T_ 2. The first electronically recorded album was *Cake Walking Babies*.

_F_ 3. Smith was the first woman to sing the blues.

_T_ 4. Grandpa Russell bid on an album signed by Coltrane.

Read the question, and write your answer.

What was the relationship between Smith and Gertrude "Ma" Rainey? **Rainey was the first woman to sing the blues; Smith worked with Rainey in a traveling show; Rainey may have coached Smith.**

Express Yourself • Book 3   43

Bidding on the Past

Thinking and Writing

Name _____ Date _____

Bidding on the Past
Think About It

Write about or give an oral presentation for each question.

1. Compare your favorite kind of music with jazz and blues. In what ways are the three music styles similar? **Answers will vary.**

2. How is improvisation like scat? How are they different? **Improvisation is to make up music while playing; *scat* is to make up words or syllables while singing. Scat is only used for singing, but improvisation can be done by instrument or voice.**

3. Compare Armstrong with Fitzgerald. How did each of them change music and the culture around them? Which do you think had more impact? **Answers will vary.**

4. Regine saw people of all races and ages at the auction. Why do you think jazz and blues appeal to such a wide variety of people? **Accept reasonable answers.**

Write About It

Choose one of the questions below. Write your answer on a sheet of paper.

1. Think about ways slavery shaped blues and jazz. How did blues and jazz impact the civil rights movement? Use your ideas to write a newspaper-style article about the important place music has in U.S. culture and history.

2. Based on this story, write a three-paragraph description of jazz and blues. Include a paragraph about the history of these two types of music. When you are done, listen to songs by three of the jazz and blues artists you read about in this book. Now write three new paragraphs describing jazz and blues. How did your understanding of the music change after hearing it?

3. Complete the Main Idea/Details Chart for this book.

44   Express Yourself • Book 3

Bidding on the Past

Express Yourself • Book 3   47

Building Background

Name _____ Date _____

Blues King: The Story of B. B. King
What You Know

Write answers to these questions.

1. What different types of music are there? What distinguishes one type from another? _____

2. Why do you think people say they feel "blue" when they are sad? What do you think "blues" music is? _____

3. What does it mean to be the "king" of something? _____
_____

4. Sometimes song lyrics tell the story of a group of people or a single person. Why do you think this occurs? Name a few songs and describe the stories they tell. _____
_____

5. Who is your favorite musician? What is your favorite musical group? Why do you like them? _____

Word Meanings
Matching

Look for these words as you read your chapter book. When you find a word, draw a line to connect the word with the correct definition.

inducted   a large farm, usually in a warm climate, on which the farm workers live

kerosene   formally admitted to a position or organization

legend   a thin oil, made mainly from petroleum, that is used as a fuel

plantation   a slightly trembling effect given to a vocal or instrumental tone by slight and rapid variations in pitch

vibrato   an extremely famous person, especially in a particular field

Word Lists

Blues King: The Story of B. B. King

	Unfamiliar Words	Word Meanings	Proper Nouns
Chapter 1	celebrated famous guitar honor	legend	Lucille
Chapter 2	borrow cousin electric machines owed profit segregated separated sharecroppers soul stuttered style	plantation	Beale Street Blind Lemon Jefferson Bukka White Cartledge Chicago Indianola Itta Bena Johnson Barrett Kilmichael Lonnie Johnson Memphis Mississippi Riley B. King Tennessee
Chapter 3	agency business divorce emotions excitement health jazz neighborhood performance schedule talent tour	vibrato	Apollo Theater Elvis Presley Harlem Hawaiian Pepticon Regal Theater Sepia Swing Club
Chapter 4	concert developed magazine marriage old-fashioned ovation popularity recordings titled		California England Europe San Francisco The Beatles
Chapter 5	award barrel collapse commercials including rhythm stardom	kerosene	Arkansas Bono Las Vegas Lincoln Center Nevada New York City Queen Elizabeth Russia
Chapter 6	ambassador courage diabetes exactly medication overweight raise taught	inducted	Delta Interpretive Center Elton John Gloria Estefan

Express Yourself • Book 4

Chapter Quiz

Name _____ Date _____

Blues King: The Story of B. B. King
Chapter 1, "King of the Blues"

Mark each statement *T* for true or *F* for false.

_____ 1. B. B. King is one of the most popular blues guitarists in the world.

_____ 2. When King celebrated his 80th birthday in 2005, he had been playing music for almost 30 years.

_____ 3. King's guitar, named Luanne, is as famous as he is.

_____ 4. King is often called the "King of the Blues" because he is one of the best guitar players in the world, and he is a living legend.

_____ 5. King learned to play the guitar when he was a child.

_____ 6. King grew up picking cotton on his parents' farm.

_____ 7. Although King is one of the greatest guitar players in the world, for many years most Americans had never heard of him.

_____ 8. For many years King played only for African American audiences.

_____ 9. King believes that blues musicians should pass on myths and legends from long ago.

_____ 10. King once said blues singers tell stories "about things we like, things we dislike, things we wish, and things we wish would not be."

Read the question, and write your answer.

What events in King's life might have shaped the stories he tried to tell through blues music? _____

_____

_____

Chapter Quiz

Name _____ Date _____

Blues King: The Story of B. B. King
Chapter 2, "Blues All around Me"

Number the events in order from 1 to 5.

___ King was born on a cotton plantation in Itta Bena, Mississippi.

___ King borrowed 15 dollars and bought his first guitar.

___ King heard an electric guitar for the first time when he went to church with his grandmother.

___ The preacher at the church taught King how to play the guitar.

___ After his parents separated, King lived most of the time with his grandmother in Kilmichael, Mississippi.

Number the events in order from 6 to 10.

___ King returned to Kilmichael and lived with the Cartledge family.

___ King decided to move to Memphis, Tennessee, with $2.50 in his pocket and his guitar.

___ King's grandmother died, and he lived alone in her cabin.

___ King moved to Indianola, Mississippi, and found a job driving a tractor.

___ King went to live with his father and stepmother.

Read the question, and write your answer.

What events and musicians helped King develop as an artist and a musician? _____

_____

_____

Express Yourself • Book 4   51

Chapter Quiz

Name _____ Date _____

Blues King: The Story of B. B. King
Chapter 3, "Beale Street and Beyond"

Fill in the bubble beside the answer for each question.

1. Why did King want to go to Beale Street?

    Ⓐ It was known as the center of African American business and entertainment.

    Ⓑ He was tired of living in the Delta and working as a tractor driver.

    Ⓒ He wanted to find a higher-paying job.

2. Once in Memphis, King learned more about playing the blues from

    Ⓐ Bukka White, his mom's cousin.

    Ⓑ many different blues musicians who practiced and performed in Memphis.

    Ⓒ both A and B

3. King returned to Indianola after ten months because he

    Ⓐ missed his wife.

    Ⓑ lost his job working as a DJ at a radio station.

    Ⓒ felt he would never be a successful musician.

4. For King, living and working in Memphis was a way to

    Ⓐ work and record songs with Elvis Presley.

    Ⓑ improve his guitar skills and develop an audience for his music.

    Ⓒ get a job with one of the old-time blues bands.

Read the question, and write your answer.

How did King keep his music from being a copy of blues musicians like White? _____

_____

52   Express Yourself • Book 4

Chapter Quiz

Name _____ Date _____

Blues King: The Story of B. B. King
Chapter 4, "Rock and Roll"

Mark each statement *T* for true or *F* for false.

____ 1. By the early 1960s, blues music was not very popular.

____ 2. King continued to tour and was very popular with his audiences.

____ 3. During the early 1960s, King was booed while performing because the audience felt his music was too "old."

____ 4. Many blues musicians went to Europe to play and developed new audiences.

____ 5. Jazz musicians, including The Beatles and The Who, copied and developed their own blues styles.

Number the events in order from 1 to 5.

____ The Rolling Stones asked King to be their opening act for a tour in North America.

____ King received a standing ovation at a concert hall in San Francisco, California.

____ King recorded the album *Live at the Regal*.

____ Eric Clapton told *Rolling Stone* magazine he didn't think there was a better blues guitarist in the world than King.

____ King's song "The Thrill Is Gone" became a hit, and King began to play on college campuses.

Read the question, and write your answer.

Explain what is meant by the song title, "The Blues Had a Baby, and They Named It Rock and Roll." _____

_____

Express Yourself • Book 4

Chapter Quiz

Name _____ Date _____

Blues King: The Story of B. B. King
Chapter 5, "Stardom"

Fill in the bubble beside the answer for each question.

1. King never stopped working because he
   - Ⓐ needed the money.
   - Ⓑ wanted to keep his music in front of people.
   - Ⓒ wanted to become the best rock-and-roll guitar player ever.

2. Because King wanted young people to learn about the blues, he
   - Ⓐ recorded with a wide range of musicians.
   - Ⓑ appeared on television shows and in commercials.
   - Ⓒ both A and B

3. Which album sold more than any other album King made?
   - Ⓐ *Live in Cook County Jail*
   - Ⓑ *Riding with the King*
   - Ⓒ *When Love Comes to Town*

4. Why does King name his guitars Lucille?
   - Ⓐ He wants to remind himself not to act foolishly and put himself in danger.
   - Ⓑ His mother's name was Lucille.
   - Ⓒ His grandmother, who helped raise him and introduced him to the electric guitar, was named Lucille.

Read the question, and write your answer.

What has King done to keep blues music alive? _____

_____

_____

Chapter Quiz

Name _____ Date _____

Blues King: The Story of B. B. King
Chapter 6, "Blues Ambassador"

Mark each statement *T* for true or *F* for false.

____ 1. The first B. B. King Blues Club opened in Times Square in New York City.

____ 2. *Rolling Stone* magazine has called King the greatest living guitarist.

____ 3. In 2005 work began on the B. B. King Museum in Harlem.

____ 4. In celebration of his 80th birthday, King recorded an album called *B. B. King and Friends—80* with musicians like Elton John, Clapton, and Gloria Estefan.

____ 5. King has won 14 Grammy Awards, and in 1987 he received a Lifetime Achievement Award.

____ 6. Despite his many successes, King has never been inducted into the Rock and Roll Hall of Fame.

____ 7. In 2005 President George Bush awarded King the Presidential Medal for Music.

____ 8. In 2006 King's album *Live at the Regal* became part of the Grammy Hall of Fame.

____ 9. After King played his 10,000th show he announced he was retiring.

____ 10. Although King disliked growing up during a time of segregation, he believes it taught him how to get along with all kinds of people.

Read the question, and write your answer.

How does King feel about his life? _____

_____

_____

Express Yourself • Book 4

Thinking and Writing

Name _____ Date _____

Blues King: The Story of B. B. King
Think About It

Write about or give an oral presentation for each question.

1. How did sharecropping and segregation help shape blues music?

2. What influences in King's life led him to greatness both as a blues musician and as a guitarist?

3. How many kinds of musical groups did King play with? Why do you think he played with all kinds of music groups and also made television commercials?

4. How has blues music changed over the past decades?

Write About It

Choose one of the questions below. Write your answer on a sheet of paper.

1. What southern influences appear in King's music?

2. What lesson does the story of King's life teach about determination and the human spirit?

3. How do musicians and musical groups influence each other? How does music change as a result of these interactions?

4. Complete the Book Report Form for this book.

Fluency Passages

Blues King: The Story of B. B. King

Chapter 3 *pages 18 and 19*

*King needed a new name to use on the air. First he called himself the	15
"Beale Street Blues Boy." But that was too long, so he changed it to the	30
"Blues Boy King." Finally that was shortened to "B. B. King."	41
Blues was changing too. Sharecropping came to an end as new	52
machines were invented that could do the hard work in the cotton fields.	65
Many African Americans left the Delta for cities farther north. Many blues	77
musicians moved too. A lot of them moved to Chicago.	87
In Memphis, King became more popular. Around 1949 he signed his	98
first record contract. The contract was with a company that made records	110
aimed at African American listeners. One of his first songs was called	122
"B. B. Boogie."	125
When King became a DJ,* he started listening to lots of different	137
kinds of music.	140

Chapter 6 *page 40*

*King celebrated his 80th birthday in 2005. He still tours all the time.	13
He says he tours because he rarely hears the blues on the radio. He	27
feels that if he doesn't tour, no one will listen to the blues anymore.	41
King put out an album for his 80th birthday. It was called *B. B. King*	56
and Friends—80. For the album he played songs with musicians like	68
Clapton, Elton John, Sting, U2, and Gloria Estefan.	76
He has won 14 Grammy Awards. He received a Lifetime Achievement	87
Award in 1987. He was also inducted into the Rock and Roll Hall of Fame	102
in 1987. And he was awarded a Presidential Medal of the Arts in 1990. He	117
has made over 70 albums in his career, and he has sold over* 40 million	132
records.	133

- The target rate for **Express Yourself** is 130 wcpm. The asterisks (*) mark 130 words.

- Listen to the student read the passage. Count the number of words read in one minute and the number of errors.

- For the reading rate, subtract the number of errors from the total number of words read.

- Have students enter their scores on their **Fluency Graph.** See page 9.

Answer Key

Building Background

Name _____ Date _____

Blues King: The Story of B. B. King
What You Know
Write answers to these questions.

1. What different types of music are there? What distinguishes one type from another? **Accept reasonable responses.**
2. Why do you think people say they feel "blue" when they are sad? What do you think "blues" music is? **Accept reasonable responses.**
3. What does it mean to be the "king" of something? **Answers should include being a ruler, at the top, or the very best at a particular activity.**
4. Sometimes song lyrics tell the story of a group of people or a single person. Why do you think this occurs? Name a few songs and describe the stories they tell. **Answers will vary; ballads and blues usually tell stories.**
5. Who is your favorite musician? What is your favorite musical group? Why do you like them? **Answers will vary.**

Word Meanings
Matching

Look for these words as you read your chapter book. When you find a word, draw a line to connect the word with the correct definition.

- inducted — formally admitted to a position or organization
- kerosene — a thin oil, made mainly from petroleum, that is used as a fuel
- legend — an extremely famous person, especially in a particular field
- plantation — a large farm, usually in a warm climate, on which the farm workers live
- vibrato — a slightly trembling effect given to a vocal or instrumental tone by slight and rapid variations in pitch

---

Chapter Quiz

Name _____ Date _____

Blues King: The Story of B. B. King
Chapter 1, "King of the Blues"

Mark each statement *T* for true or *F* for false.

- **T** 1. B. B. King is one of the most popular blues guitarists in the world.
- **F** 2. When King celebrated his 80th birthday in 2005, he had been playing music for almost 30 years.
- **F** 3. King's guitar, named Luanne, is as famous as he is.
- **T** 4. King is often called the "King of the Blues" because he is one of the best guitar players in the world, and he is a living legend.
- **T** 5. King learned to play the guitar when he was a child.
- **F** 6. King grew up picking cotton on his parents' farm.
- **T** 7. Although King is one of the greatest guitar players in the world, for many years most Americans had never heard of him.
- **T** 8. For many years King played only for African American audiences.
- **F** 9. King believes that blues musicians should pass on myths and legends from long ago.
- **T** 10. King once said blues singers tell stories "about things we like, things we dislike, things we wish, and things we wish would not be."

Read the question, and write your answer.

What events in King's life might have shaped the stories he tried to tell through blues music? **growing up poor, taking care of himself**

Chapter Quiz

Name _____ Date _____

Blues King: The Story of B. B. King
Chapter 2, "Blues All around Me"

Number the events in order from 1 to 5.

- **1** King was born on a cotton plantation in Itta Bena, Mississippi.
- **5** King borrowed 15 dollars and bought his first guitar.
- **3** King heard an electric guitar for the first time when he went to church with his grandmother.
- **4** The preacher at the church taught King how to play the guitar.
- **2** After his parents separated, King lived most of the time with his grandmother in Kilmichael, Mississippi.

Number the events in order from 6 to 10.

- **8** King returned to Kilmichael and lived with the Cartledge family.
- **10** King decided to move to Memphis, Tennessee, with $2.50 in his pocket and his guitar.
- **6** King's grandmother died, and he lived alone in her cabin.
- **9** King moved to Indianola, Mississippi, and found a job driving a tractor.
- **7** King went to live with his father and stepmother.

Read the question, and write your answer.

What events and musicians helped King develop as an artist and a musician? **Ideas: growing up poor, segregation, sharecropping, his preacher, learning to play the electric guitar, listening to Blind Lemon Jefferson, Lonnie Johnson, and T-Bone Walker**

Chapter Quiz

Name _____ Date _____

Blues King: The Story of B. B. King
Chapter 3, "Beale Street and Beyond"

Fill in the bubble beside the answer for each question.

1. Why did King want to go to Beale Street?
   - ● It was known as the center of African American business and entertainment.
   - Ⓑ He was tired of living in the Delta and working as a tractor driver.
   - Ⓒ He wanted to find a higher-paying job.

2. Once in Memphis, King learned more about playing the blues from
   - Ⓐ Bukka White, his mom's cousin.
   - Ⓑ many different blues musicians who practiced and performed in Memphis.
   - ● both A and B

3. King returned to Indianola after ten months because he
   - ● missed his wife.
   - Ⓑ lost his job working as a DJ at a radio station.
   - Ⓒ felt he would never be a successful musician.

4. For King, living and working in Memphis was a way to
   - Ⓐ work and record songs with Elvis Presley.
   - ● improve his guitar skills and develop an audience for his music.
   - Ⓒ get a job with one of the old-time blues bands.

Read the question, and write your answer.

How did King keep his music from being a copy of blues musicians like White? **King listened to different kinds and styles of music, brought many different sounds together, and created his own new sound.**

---

58   Express Yourself • Book 4

Answer Key

Chapter Quiz

Name _____ Date _____

Blues King: The Story of B. B. King
Chapter 4, "Rock and Roll"

Mark each statement *T* for true or *F* for false.

__T__ 1. By the early 1960s, blues music was not very popular.

__F__ 2. King continued to tour and was very popular with his audiences.

__T__ 3. During the early 1960s, King was booed while performing because the audience felt his music was too "old."

__T__ 4. Many blues musicians went to Europe to play and developed new audiences.

__F__ 5. Jazz musicians, including The Beatles and The Who, copied and developed their own blues styles.

Number the events in order from 1 to 5.

__4__ The Rolling Stones asked King to be their opening act for a tour in North America.

__2__ King received a standing ovation at a concert hall in San Francisco, California.

__1__ King recorded the album *Live at the Regal*.

__3__ Eric Clapton told *Rolling Stone* magazine he didn't think there was a better blues guitarist in the world than King.

__5__ King's song "The Thrill Is Gone" became a hit, and King began to play on college campuses.

Read the question, and write your answer.

Explain what is meant by the song title, "The Blues Had a Baby, and They Named It Rock and Roll." __Rock and roll musicians copied blues music and then developed their own blues styles.__

Express Yourself • Book 4   53

Blues King: The Story of B. B. King

Chapter Quiz

Name _____ Date _____

Blues King: The Story of B. B. King
Chapter 5, "Stardom"

Fill in the bubble beside the answer for each question.

1. King never stopped working because he
   Ⓐ needed the money.
   ● wanted to keep his music in front of people.
   Ⓒ wanted to become the best rock-and-roll guitar player ever.

2. Because King wanted young people to learn about the blues, he
   Ⓐ recorded with a wide range of musicians.
   Ⓑ appeared on television shows and in commercials.
   ● both A and B

3. Which album sold more than any other album King made?
   Ⓐ *Live in Cook County Jail*
   ● *Riding with the King*
   Ⓒ *When Love Comes to Town*

4. Why does King name his guitars Lucille?
   ● He wants to remind himself not to act foolishly and put himself in danger.
   Ⓑ His mother's name was Lucille.
   Ⓒ His grandmother, who helped raise him and introduced him to the electric guitar, was named Lucille.

Read the question, and write your answer.

What has King done to keep blues music alive? __Ideas: played with rock bands and rock stars; played on college campuses, in clubs, large theaters, on television; appeared in commercials__

54   Express Yourself • Book 4

Blues King: The Story of B. B. King

Chapter Quiz

Name _____ Date _____

Blues King: The Story of B. B. King
Chapter 6, "Blues Ambassador"

Mark each statement *T* for true or *F* for false.

__F__ 1. The first B. B. King Blues Club opened in Times Square in New York City.

__T__ 2. *Rolling Stone* magazine has called King the greatest living guitarist.

__F__ 3. In 2005 work began on the B. B. King Museum in Harlem.

__T__ 4. In celebration of his 80th birthday, King recorded an album called *B. B. King and Friends—80* with musicians like Elton John, Clapton, and Gloria Estefan.

__T__ 5. King has won 14 Grammy Awards, and in 1987 he received a Lifetime Achievement Award.

__F__ 6. Despite his many successes, King has never been inducted into the Rock and Roll Hall of Fame.

__F__ 7. In 2005 President George Bush awarded King the Presidential Medal for Music.

__T__ 8. In 2006 King's album *Live at the Regal* became part of the Grammy Hall of Fame.

__F__ 9. After King played his 10,000th show he announced he was retiring.

__T__ 10. Although King disliked growing up during a time of segregation, he believes it taught him how to get along with all kinds of people.

Read the question, and write your answer.

How does King feel about his life? __Accept reasonable responses.__

Express Yourself • Book 4   55

Blues King: The Story of B. B. King

Thinking and Writing

Name _____ Date _____

Blues King: The Story of B. B. King
Think About It

Write about or give an oral presentation for each question.

1. How did sharecropping and segregation help shape blues music? __Blues songs often speak of poverty, sadness, and hard times.__

2. What influences in King's life led him to greatness both as a blues musician and as a guitarist? __Ideas: growing up in the South, determination, hard work__

3. How many kinds of musical groups did King play with? Why do you think he played with all kinds of music groups and also made television commercials? __Answers should include country, jazz, rock, and rap; accept reasonable responses.__

4. How has blues music changed over the past decades? __Answers will vary.__

Write About It

Choose one of the questions below. Write your answer on a sheet of paper.

1. What southern influences appear in King's music?

2. What lesson does the story of King's life teach about determination and the human spirit?

3. How do musicians and musical groups influence each other? How does music change as a result of these interactions?

4. Complete the Book Report Form for this book.

56   Express Yourself • Book 4

Blues King: The Story of B. B. King

Express Yourself • Book 4   59

Building Background

Name _____ Date _____

Sports Superstars
What You Know

Write answers to these questions.

1. What traits do sports champions have in common? How do you think someone becomes a real champion? Explain your answer.
   _____

2. Do you think male athletes are more competitive than female athletes? Explain your answer. _____

3. Why do you think athletes train their minds as well as their bodies?
   _____
   _____

4. Describe two athletes whose accomplishments on and off the field have made them true champions. _____
   _____

Word Meanings
Synonyms and Antonyms

Look for these words as you read your chapter book. When you find a word, write a synonym or antonym for the word.

Synonyms

amazing: _____

champion: _____

traditional: _____

Antonyms

equal: _____

famous: _____

worse: _____

Word Lists

Sports Superstars

	Unfamiliar Words	Word Meanings	Proper Nouns
Chapter 1	amazed athlete magazines scholarship statue	equal famous	Australia California Donna de Varona Duke Kahanamoku [kah-hah-nah-MOH-koo] English Channel Gertrude Ederle [ED-er-lee] Hawaii Olympics
Chapter 2	judges style	champion	Dorothy Hamill Kristi Yamaguchi Norway Sonja Henie
Chapter 3	court doubles title trendsetter uncle	traditional	Australian Open Billie Jean King Bobby Riggs French Open Ivan Lendl Michael Chang Rosie Casals Serena Williams Venus Williams Wimbledon
Chapter 4	disease hurdles inducted success	worse	Gail Devers Pine Ridge Indian Reservation South Dakota Tunisia University of Kansas
Chapter 5	award bowl chose neighborhood professional proved	amazing	Chamique Holdsclaw [shah-MEEK-wah] Cincinnati Los Angeles Milwaukee Nancy Lieberman New York City Old Dominion Oscar Robertson Tennessee Washington Mystics
Chapter 6	charities raises		Alabama Brazil Edson Arantes do Nascimento [ED-juh-sohn ah-RAHN-tees doo nah-see-MEN-toh] Garrett Mia Hamm Pelé

Express Yourself • Book 5

Chapter Quiz

Name _____ Date _____

Sports Superstars
Chapter 1, "Making a Splash"

Fill in the bubble beside the answer for each question.

1. What did Duke Kahanamoku do when he realized that he was winning the 1912 Olympic 100-meter race?

    Ⓐ speed up

    Ⓑ slow down

    Ⓒ quit the race

2. Kahanamoku introduced people around the world to the sport of

    Ⓐ surfing.

    Ⓑ swimming.

    Ⓒ boating.

3. What caused Trudy Ederle to decide to become a swimmer?

    Ⓐ She was the best in her swimming classes at the city pool.

    Ⓑ She swam fast enough to break records.

    Ⓒ She got mad when someone made fun of the way she swam.

4. What did Ederle do that no woman had ever done before?

    Ⓐ She swam across the English Channel.

    Ⓑ She swam in rough, choppy seawater.

    Ⓒ She swam in the city pool in a two-piece bathing suit.

Read the question, and write your answer.

What character traits made Donna de Varona a successful athlete?

_____

_____

Chapter Quiz

Name _____ Date _____

Sports Superstars
Chapter 2, "Skating for Gold"

Number the events in order from 1 to 5.

____ Sonja Henie won an Olympic gold medal.

____ Henie competed in the Olympics at age 11.

____ Henie starred in the movie *One in a Million*.

____ Dorothy Hamill won an Olympic gold medal.

____ Hamill invented the "Hamill Camel."

Mark each statement *T* for true or *F* for false.

____ 1. Kristi Yamaguchi was inspired by Henie.

____ 2. Yamaguchi got up at four in the morning to practice skating before school.

____ 3. Yamaguchi never met Hamill.

____ 4. Yamaguchi fell during her Olympic routine.

____ 5. Yamaguchi won the Olympic gold medal.

Read the question, and write your answer.

What were three of the things all three skaters—Henie, Hamill, and Yamaguchi—had in common? _____

_____

_____

Express Yourself • Book 5

Chapter Quiz

Name _____ Date _____

Sports Superstars
Chapter 3, "Serving Up Greatness"

Number the events in order from 1 to 5.

____ Billie Jean King defeated Bobby Riggs as 50 million people watched the televised match.

____ Rosie Casals wore a purple and white tennis dress to Wimbledon.

____ King won Wimbledon for the first time.

____ King and Casals fought for more prize money in women's tennis.

____ King bought her first tennis racket with money she earned doing chores.

Number the events in order from 6 to 10.

____ Michael Chang lost a tennis match to his father.

____ Venus and Serena Williams became the top tennis players in Southern California under age 12.

____ Chang became the youngest male to win the French Open.

____ Venus Williams won both the U.S. Open and Wimbledon.

____ Serena Williams won the U.S. Open.

Read the question, and write your answer.

Why did Casals almost lose her chance to play at Wimbledon in 1972?

_____

_____

_____

64 Express Yourself • Book 5

Chapter Quiz

Name _____ Date _____

Sports Superstars
Chapter 4, "Runaway Successes"

Fill in the bubble beside the answer for each question.

1. To improve his skills as a long distance runner, Billy Mills
   - Ⓐ attended a school for Native Americans.
   - Ⓑ began running on the Pine Ridge Indian Reservation.
   - Ⓒ trained both his mind and body.

2. What Olympic event did Mills enter?
   - Ⓐ high-jump
   - Ⓑ 10,000-meter race
   - Ⓒ 100-meter hurdles

3. When an Australian runner bumped into Mills during his Olympic race,
   - Ⓐ Mills fell behind.
   - Ⓑ Mills kept telling himself he could still win the race.
   - Ⓒ both A and B

4. In high school, Gail Devers set records in
   - Ⓐ hurdles.
   - Ⓑ the long jump.
   - Ⓒ both A and B

5. What kept Devers from the Olympics after her 1988 American record in the 100-meter hurdles?
   - Ⓐ her studies at the University of California
   - Ⓑ Graves' disease
   - Ⓒ severe weight loss

Read the question, and write your answer.

What was Devers's greatest achievement? _____

_____

Express Yourself • Book 5

Chapter Quiz

Name _____ Date _____

Sports Superstars
Chapter 5, "Swish!"

Number the events in order from 1 to 5.

____ Oscar Robertson played for the U.S. Men's Olympic Basketball Team.

____ Robertson received a basketball scholarship to the University of Cincinnati.

____ Robertson played basketball with old cans and tennis balls.

____ Robertson was inducted into the Basketball Hall of Fame.

____ Robertson helped the Milwaukee Bucks win the NBA championship.

Mark each statement *T* for true or *F* for false.

____ 1. Nancy Lieberman's mom told her basketball was a healthy hobby.

____ 2. Lieberman was a member of the first U.S. Women's Olympic Basketball Team.

____ 3. Lieberman helped Old Dominion University win four national championships.

____ 4. Chamique Holdsclaw was taller than most of the kids in her neighborhood.

____ 5. Holdsclaw played on the U.S. Women's Olympic Basketball Team; she also played for the Washington Mystics and the Los Angeles Sparks.

Read the question, and write your answer.

What do Robertson, Lieberman, and Holdsclaw have in common?

_____

Chapter Quiz

Name _____ Date _____

Sports Superstars
Chapter 6, "Just for Kicks"

Mark each statement *T* for true or *F* for false.

____ 1. Pelé was playing professional soccer by age 15.

____ 2. Pelé invented a kick called the "motorbike kick."

____ 3. Pelé scored goals with his head.

____ 4. Pelé did not see well out of the corners of his eyes.

____ 5. Pelé helped Argentina's soccer team win three World Cup championships.

____ 6. Mia Hamm became the youngest player on the U.S. Women's National Team at age 15.

____ 7. Hamm was part of the U.S. Women's National Team that won the first Women's World Cup.

____ 8. Despite other successes, Hamm's team never won an Olympic gold medal.

____ 9. Hamm founded the Mia Hamm Foundation to help girls become professional soccer players.

____ 10. No other soccer player has scored as many goals as Hamm in international matches.

Read the question, and write your answer.

How has Hamm helped make soccer popular in the United States?

_____

_____

_____

Express Yourself • Book 5

Thinking and Writing

Name _____ Date _____

Sports Superstars
Think About It

Write about or give an oral presentation for each question.

1. Which sports superstar do you believe is the most courageous? Why?

2. Which sports superstar is the best role model for young people? Explain your answer. _____

3. Which sports superstar has done the most for women in sports?

4. Which sports superstar do you believe is the best athlete? Explain your answer. _____

Write About It

Choose one of the questions below. Write your answer on a sheet of paper.

1. Imagine that the author has asked you to suggest two famous athletes that she might feature in a sequel to this book. Which athletes would you suggest and why?

2. Hamill gave Yamaguchi important advice. Tell about the most important advice you've ever received. Explain what happened and why this advice proved to be so important.

3. Write a newspaper article about one of the athletes discussed in this book. You may wish to conduct outside research to learn more about your chosen athlete.

4. Complete the Compare and Contrast Chart for this book.

Fluency Passages

Sports Superstars

Chapter 1 *pages 4 and 5*

*The English Channel is the body of water between France and	11
England. It is 21 miles wide. Swimming it was something no woman had	24
ever done.	26
Ederle began her swim early on August 6, 1926. Some people were	38
shocked when they saw her. Back then, women wore long dresses when	50
they swam. These outfits were very heavy when they got wet. But Ederle	63
wore a lighter, two-piece outfit.	68
Ederle's arms and legs soon went stiff in the chilly water. The sea was	82
rough and choppy too. It made Ederle feel sick. But she forced herself to	96
keep going.	98
The swim took her over 14 hours. It was night by the time she finished.	113
But she had done something no other woman had done.	123
She had set a new record too.* She swam the Channel two hours faster	137
than anyone else ever had.	142

Chapter 4 *pages 26 and 27*

*The runners waited at the starting line. The starting shot rang out,	12
and the race began! The Australian and the Tunisian were in front. But	25
Mills kept up with them.	30
Near the end of the race, all three runners tried to take the lead. The	45
Australian bumped into Mills. This caused Mills to fall behind. But he kept	58
thinking, "I can win... I can win... I can win." He passed the other two	73
runners and won the race!	78
The crowd sat in shocked silence for a moment. No one thought Mills	91
could win. A reporter walked up to Mills. The first thing the reporter	104
wanted to know was who Mills was.	111
But it wasn't long before everyone knew Mills's name. His win was	123
one of the biggest upsets in Olympic* history. He also set an Olympic	136
record for the event.	140

- The target rate for **Express Yourself** is 130 wcpm. The asterisks (*) mark 130 words.

- Listen to the student read the passage. Count the number of words read in one minute and the number of errors.

- For the reading rate, subtract the number of errors from the total number of words read.

- Have students enter their scores on their **Fluency Graph.** See page 9.

Answer Key

Building Background

Name _____ Date _____

Sports Superstars
What You Know
Write answers to these questions.

1. What traits do sports champions have in common? How do you think someone becomes a real champion? Explain your answer.
   Accept reasonable responses.

2. Do you think male athletes are more competitive than female athletes? Explain your answer. **Accept reasonable responses.**

3. Why do you think athletes train their minds as well as their bodies?
   Ideas: Mental toughness and endurance are just as important as physical toughness.

4. Describe two athletes whose accomplishments on and off the field have made them true champions. **Answers will vary.**

Word Meanings
Synonyms and Antonyms
Look for these words as you read your chapter book. When you find a word, write a synonym or antonym for the word.

Synonyms
amazing: **astonishing, stunning**
champion: **winner, titleholder**
traditional: **customary, standard**

Antonyms
equal: **discriminatory, unfair**
famous: **unknown, obscure**
worse: **improved**

60 — Express Yourself • Book 5

Chapter Quiz

Name _____ Date _____

Sports Superstars
Chapter 1, "Making a Splash"
Fill in the bubble beside the answer for each question.

1. What did Duke Kahanamoku do when he realized that he was winning the 1912 Olympic 100-meter race?
   - Ⓐ speed up
   - ● slow down
   - Ⓒ quit the race

2. Kahanamoku introduced people around the world to the sport of
   - ● surfing.
   - Ⓑ swimming.
   - Ⓒ boating.

3. What caused Trudy Ederle to decide to become a swimmer?
   - Ⓐ She was the best in her swimming classes at the city pool.
   - Ⓑ She swam fast enough to break records.
   - ● She got mad when someone made fun of the way she swam.

4. What did Ederle do that no woman had ever done before?
   - ● She swam across the English Channel.
   - Ⓑ She swam in rough, choppy seawater.
   - Ⓒ She swam in the city pool in a two-piece bathing suit.

Read the question, and write your answer.

What character traits made Donna de Varona a successful athlete?
Ideas: She was determined and insisted on being an athlete despite gender barriers; she was creative because she figured out a way to pay for college when she was denied a scholarship; she was competitive.

62 — Express Yourself • Book 5

Chapter Quiz

Name _____ Date _____

Sports Superstars
Chapter 2, "Skating for Gold"
Number the events in order from 1 to 5.

- **2** Sonja Henie won an Olympic gold medal.
- **1** Henie competed in the Olympics at age 11.
- **3** Henie starred in the movie *One in a Million*.
- **5** Dorothy Hamill won an Olympic gold medal.
- **4** Hamill invented the "Hamill Camel."

Mark each statement *T* for true or *F* for false.

- **F** 1. Kristi Yamaguchi was inspired by Henie.
- **T** 2. Yamaguchi got up at four in the morning to practice skating before school.
- **F** 3. Yamaguchi never met Hamill.
- **T** 4. Yamaguchi fell during her Olympic routine.
- **T** 5. Yamaguchi won the Olympic gold medal.

Read the question, and write your answer.

What were three of the things all three skaters—Henie, Hamill, and Yamaguchi—had in common? **Ideas: practiced hard; started young; skated in the Olympics; added exciting spins and jumps to their routines**

Express Yourself • Book 5 — 63

Chapter Quiz

Name _____ Date _____

Sports Superstars
Chapter 3, "Serving Up Greatness"
Number the events in order from 1 to 5.

- **5** Billie Jean King defeated Bobby Riggs as 50 million people watched the televised match.
- **3** Rosie Casals wore a purple and white tennis dress to Wimbledon.
- **2** King won Wimbledon for the first time.
- **4** King and Casals fought for more prize money in women's tennis.
- **1** King bought her first tennis racket with money she earned doing chores.

Number the events in order from 6 to 10.

- **6** Michael Chang lost a tennis match to his father.
- **8** Venus and Serena Williams became the top tennis players in Southern California under age 12.
- **7** Chang became the youngest male to win the French Open.
- **10** Venus Williams won both the U.S. Open and Wimbledon.
- **9** Serena Williams won the U.S. Open.

Read the question, and write your answer.

Why did Casals almost lose her chance to play at Wimbledon in 1972?
She wore a purple and white tennis dress instead of the traditional "tennis whites."

64 — Express Yourself • Book 5

---

70 — Express Yourself • Book 5

Answer Key

Chapter Quiz

Name _____ Date _____

Sports Superstars
Chapter 4, "Runaway Successes"
Fill in the bubble beside the answer for each question.

1. To improve his skills as a long distance runner, Billy Mills
   - Ⓐ attended a school for Native Americans.
   - Ⓑ began running on the Pine Ridge Indian Reservation.
   - ● trained both his mind and body.

2. What Olympic event did Mills enter?
   - Ⓐ high-jump
   - ● 10,000-meter race
   - Ⓒ 100-meter hurdles

3. When an Australian runner bumped into Mills during his Olympic race,
   - Ⓐ Mills fell behind.
   - Ⓑ Mills kept telling himself he could still win the race.
   - ● both A and B

4. In high school, Gail Devers set records in
   - ● hurdles.
   - Ⓑ the long jump.
   - Ⓒ both A and B

5. What kept Devers from the Olympics after her 1988 American record in the 100-meter hurdles?
   - Ⓐ her studies at the University of California
   - ● Graves' disease
   - Ⓒ severe weight loss

Read the question, and write your answer.
What was Devers's greatest achievement? **Ideas: Olympic gold medals; her triumph over Graves' disease**

Express Yourself • Book 5   65

Sports Superstars

Chapter Quiz

Name _____ Date _____

Sports Superstars
Chapter 5, "Swish!"
Number the events in order from 1 to 5.

_3_ Oscar Robertson played for the U.S. Men's Olympic Basketball Team.
_2_ Robertson received a basketball scholarship to the University of Cincinnati.
_1_ Robertson played basketball with old cans and tennis balls.
_5_ Robertson was inducted into the Basketball Hall of Fame.
_4_ Robertson helped the Milwaukee Bucks win the NBA championship.

Mark each statement *T* for true or *F* for false.

_F_ 1. Nancy Lieberman's mom told her basketball was a healthy hobby.
_T_ 2. Lieberman was a member of the first U.S. Women's Olympic Basketball Team.
_F_ 3. Lieberman helped Old Dominion University win four national championships.
_F_ 4. Chamique Holdsclaw was taller than most of the kids in her neighborhood.
_T_ 5. Holdsclaw played on the U.S. Women's Olympic Basketball Team; she also played for the Washington Mystics and the Los Angeles Sparks.

Read the question, and write your answer.
What do Robertson, Lieberman, and Holdsclaw have in common?
Ideas: good all-around players; played in college; on Olympic teams; played professionally; high statistics in scoring, rebounding, and assisting

66   Express Yourself • Book 5

Sports Superstars

Chapter Quiz

Name _____ Date _____

Sports Superstars
Chapter 6, "Just for Kicks"
Mark each statement *T* for true or *F* for false.

_T_ 1. Pelé was playing professional soccer by age 15.
_F_ 2. Pelé invented a kick called the "motorbike kick."
_T_ 3. Pelé scored goals with his head.
_F_ 4. Pelé did not see well out of the corners of his eyes.
_F_ 5. Pelé helped Argentina's soccer team win three World Cup championships.
_T_ 6. Mia Hamm became the youngest player on the U.S. Women's National Team at age 15.
_T_ 7. Hamm was part of the U.S. Women's National Team that won the first Women's World Cup.
_F_ 8. Despite other successes, Hamm's team never won an Olympic gold medal.
_F_ 9. Hamm founded the Mia Hamm Foundation to help girls become professional soccer players.
_T_ 10. No other soccer player has scored as many goals as Hamm in international matches.

Read the question, and write your answer.
How has Hamm helped make soccer popular in the United States?
Ideas: U.S. wins at the Women's World Cup and the Olympics got people interested in the sport; Hamm's interviews and television ad with Michael Jordan brought soccer into popular culture.

Express Yourself • Book 5   67

Sports Superstars

Thinking and Writing

Name _____ Date _____

Sports Superstars
Think About It
Write about or give an oral presentation for each question.

1. Which sports superstar do you believe is the most courageous? Why? **Answers will vary.**

2. Which sports superstar is the best role model for young people? Explain your answer. **Answers will vary.**

3. Which sports superstar has done the most for women in sports? **Idea: King because she directly confronted prejudice and inequalities**

4. Which sports superstar do you believe is the best athlete? Explain your answer. **Answers will vary.**

Write About It
Choose one of the questions below. Write your answer on a sheet of paper.

1. Imagine that the author has asked you to suggest two famous athletes that she might feature in a sequel to this book. Which athletes would you suggest and why?

2. Hamill gave Yamaguchi important advice. Tell about the most important advice you've ever received. Explain what happened and why this advice proved to be so important.

3. Write a newspaper article about one of the athletes discussed in this book. You may wish to conduct outside research to learn more about your chosen athlete.

4. Complete the Compare and Contrast Chart for this book.

68   Express Yourself • Book 5

Sports Superstars

Express Yourself • Book 5   71

Building Background

Name _____ Date _____

Art for All!
What You Know

Write answers to these questions.

1. Why do you think people like to paint or create sculptures?
   _____

2. Describe a mural you have seen on a building or wall. What do you think is the purpose of the mural? _____
   _____

3. Think of a piece of art you have seen outside, such as a statue or sculpture. Describe it and tell whether or not you like it. Explain your reasons. _____
   _____

4. If you visited an art museum, what kinds of art would you expect to see there? How might the art inside the museum differ from art you might see outside at a park or in a public garden?
   _____
   _____

Word Meanings
Definitions

Look for these words as you read your chapter book. When you find one of these words, write its definition.

ancient: _____

fresco: _____

cattle: _____

polished: _____

sewing machine: _____

umbrella: _____

Word Lists

Art for All!

	Unfamiliar Words	Word Meanings	Proper Nouns
Chapter 1	example famous fountain include including statue woolly mammoths	ancient	Africa Bolivia Chauvet Cave [shoh-VAY] Consquer Cave [kohn-SKAY] France French India Spain
Chapter 2	create encourage machine mural	fresco	Albuquerque California Diego Rivera Florida Los Angeles Mexico Miami-Dade New Mexico Ohio Olympic Oregon South Carolina Vermont
Chapter 3	chose community healthy objects special warn	cattle	
Chapter 4	affect diamond focused honor meant volunteers	polished	Athens Chinese Frederick Hart Glenna Goodacre Maya Lin Three Servicemen Statue Vietnam Veterans Memorial Washington Yale University
Chapter 5			Federal Plaza New York City Richard Serra *Tilted Arc*
Chapter 6	models project unwrapped wrap	sewing machine umbrella	Arkansas Australia Berlin Bulgaria Christo Javacheff Colorado Germany Japan Jeanne-Claude Javacheff [yah-VAH-shef] Kansas City Missouri Morocco Paris

Express Yourself • Book 6

73

Chapter Quiz

Name _____ Date _____

Art for All!
Chapter 1, "Public Art Rocks"

Fill in the bubble beside the answer for each question.

1. Public art is art that
   - Ⓐ is created by the public.
   - Ⓑ is displayed in a public place.
   - Ⓒ stays inside a museum so the public can enjoy it for a very long time.

2. Cave art has been found in
   - Ⓐ France and Spain.
   - Ⓑ South America, India, and Africa.
   - Ⓒ both A and B

3. Most cave paintings show
   - Ⓐ animals.
   - Ⓑ people doing daily work.
   - Ⓒ objects people used long ago.

4. Why do many old rock paintings in Mexico still exist?
   - Ⓐ People have protected the art.
   - Ⓑ Artists have restored the paintings.
   - Ⓒ The dry desert air has helped protect the paintings.

Read the question, and write your answer.

Why do you think people painted on cave walls? _____

_____

_____

Chapter Quiz

Name _____ Date _____

Art for All!
Chapter 2, "Fresh Public Art"

Mark each statement *T* for true or *F* for false.

___ 1. Diego Rivera was born in New Mexico.

___ 2. Rivera wanted his murals to show poor people how wealthy people lived.

___ 3. Rivera painted huge murals in cities across America.

___ 4. Rivera's art led to an important mural movement.

___ 5. There are still a lot of Rivera-style murals in the northeastern United States.

___ 6. People have to know a lot about art to understand Rivera's murals.

___ 7. Only a few cities have public art programs.

___ 8. Albuquerque, New Mexico, has had a public art program for many years.

___ 9. Some murals along the freeways in Miami-Dade, Florida, were painted for the 1984 Summer Olympic Games.

___ 10. Public art programs are found only in the Southwest.

Read the question, and write your answer.

How did Rivera's murals help Mexican workers? _____

_____

_____

Express Yourself • Book 6   75

Chapter Quiz

Name _____ Date _____

Art for All!
Chapter 3, "Mural, Mural on the Wall"

Mark each statement *T* for true or *F* for false.

____ 1. Women in Africa have painted murals on the walls of their homes for hundreds of years.

____ 2. Most of the mural paintings in South Africa are still in homes.

____ 3. Community murals are painted by city workers.

____ 4. Like many of Rivera's murals, community murals show people working.

____ 5. Some murals are used to teach people.

____ 6. Community murals are also used to advertise businesses that serve people living in the community.

____ 7. Some large murals are painted by artists who are paid for their work.

____ 8. Paid artists are given strict instructions about what to paint.

____ 9. Murals in South Africa often show black people separated from white people.

____ 10. Murals reflect the important changes that have taken place in South Africa.

Read the question, and write your answer.

How are the murals in cities different from the murals women used to paint on their homes? _____

_____

_____

76   Express Yourself • Book 6

Chapter Quiz

Name _____ Date _____

Art for All!
Chapter 4, "The Wall"

Fill in the bubble beside the answer for each question.

1. The Vietnam Veterans Memorial is
   - Ⓐ in a park, surrounded by trees and statues.
   - Ⓑ a single, tall, black stone wall in Washington, D.C.
   - Ⓒ located in a park in New York City.

2. The design by Maya Lin
   - Ⓐ was chosen because it would be easy and inexpensive to build.
   - Ⓑ finished third in the contest.
   - Ⓒ was chosen from over 1,400 designs.

3. People who visit the Wall
   - Ⓐ often leave items there.
   - Ⓑ are not allowed to touch it.
   - Ⓒ are allowed to use paper and pencils to make rubbings of the names on it.

4. Two other Vietnam War memorials have been added
   - Ⓐ by people who were angry about the war.
   - Ⓑ because some people did not like Lin's design.
   - Ⓒ so more people would visit the memorial.

Read the question, and write your answer.

Where did the money to build the Wall come from? _____

_____

_____

Express Yourself • Book 6   77

Chapter Quiz

Name _____ Date _____

Art for All!
Chapter 5, "The Public Says, 'No!' "

Mark each statement *T* for true or *F* for false.

___ 1. Richard Serra created a piece of art for a public place.

___ 2. Serra's art was part of a public art program in New York City.

___ 3. Most people really liked his work called *Tilted Arc*.

___ 4. *Tilted Arc* was a huge stone wall, 120 feet long, designed for Central Park.

___ 5. Some people said this piece of public art kept the public from using a public place.

___ 6. A private hearing on the artwork was held.

___ 7. The hearing ruled that the artwork should be removed.

___ 8. The artist was pleased to have his work moved to a new location.

___ 9. *Tilted Arc* was cut into pieces and moved to a private location.

___ 10. The artist's rights were more important than what people liked.

Read the question, and write your answer.

What were some of the complaints people had about *Tilted Arc?*

_____

_____

_____

Chapter Quiz

Name _____ Date _____

Art for All!
Chapter 6, "Miles of Public Art"

Fill in the bubble beside the answer for each question.

1. Christo and Jeanne-Claude Javacheff are
   - Ⓐ public artists from Bolivia.
   - Ⓑ public artists who live and work in Paris.
   - Ⓒ two of the most famous public artists in the world.

2. Christo and Jeanne-Claude's public art creations
   - Ⓐ take years to plan and last a long time.
   - Ⓑ are often the same, but are displayed in different locations.
   - Ⓒ take years to plan and are on display for a brief time.

3. Some of Christo and Jeanne-Claude's artwork involved
   - Ⓐ wrapping thousands of small objects with orange fabric.
   - Ⓑ wrapping a large building in Germany.
   - Ⓒ building a wooden fence across more than 24 miles in California.

4. Who pays for the materials and workers needed for Christo and Jeanne-Claude's artwork?
   - Ⓐ The artists pay for the cost of their artwork.
   - Ⓑ Christo and Jeanne-Claude's artwork is part of a worldwide public art program.
   - Ⓒ People pay to see the artwork.

Read the question, and write your answer.

Describe the kind of artwork created by Christo and Jeanne-Claude. What is the environmental impact of their displays? _____

_____

_____

Express Yourself • Book 6

Thinking and Writing

Name _____ Date _____

Art for All!
Think About It

Write about or give an oral presentation for each question.

1. How are Rivera's murals and community murals in South Africa similar? How are they different? _____

2. How do people who visit the Vietnam Veterans Memorial interact with it? Do you think this is an important aspect of this memorial? Explain your answer. _____

3. What aspects of *Tilted Arc* took away from its role as public art?

4. Why do you think Christo and Jean-Claude only leave their work on display for about two weeks? _____

Write About It

Choose one of the questions below. Write your answer on a sheet of paper.

1. Why is public art important? How does it help people? How does it enrich our cities?

2. Write a letter to public officials in New York City asking that *Tilted Arc* be removed. In your letter, propose the type of art you would like to see in the Federal Plaza in New York.

3. If you were given the chance to choose Christo and Jeanne-Claude's next work of art, what would you suggest? Be specific and tell how it would be carried out.

4. Complete the Making Inferences Chart for this book.

Fluency Passages

Art for All!

Chapter 2 *pages 8 and 9*

*Long ago there were very few towns or places where a lot of people	14
lived together. People mostly lived with their families or in small groups.	26
When they did begin living together in towns, their lives changed. And that	39
also changed public art.	43
Diego Rivera was someone who helped change public art. He was	54
born in 1886 in Mexico. He thought that art, including public art, should do	68
more than just show what things look like. He thought art should try to	82
explain the things people face in their day-to-day lives.	91
Rivera did not like that most paintings were hidden away in museums.	103
Not many people saw those paintings. He wanted to share his art with	116
everyone. He wanted the public to see his art.	125
To share his ideas, Rivera* painted huge murals. They covered whole walls.	137

Chapter 4 *pages 24 and 25*

*The stone walls would also reflect people looking at the names on the	13
Wall. She also planned for the walls to sink into the ground at the corner,	28
like a grave.	31
Lin did not want the memorial to say who won or lost the Vietnam	45
War. She just wanted it to show that many people had lost their lives.	59
Millions of people have visited the Wall since it was built. Some come	72
to remember. Others come to learn more about the Vietnam War. Most are	85
stunned by how many names are on the Wall.	94
This memorial is meant to be seen. And it is meant to be touched. For years	110
people used paper and pencils to make rubbings of the names on the Wall.	124
They took the rubbings home to* help them remember.	133

- The target rate for **Express Yourself** is 130 wcpm. The asterisks (*) mark 130 words.
- Listen to the student read the passage. Count the number of words read in one minute and the number of errors.
- For the reading rate, subtract the number of errors from the total number of words read.
- Have students enter their scores on their **Fluency Graph.** See page 9.

Express Yourself • Book 6

Answer Key

Building Background

Name _____ Date _____

Art for All!
What You Know
Write answers to these questions.

1. Why do you think people like to paint or create sculptures?
   express ideas creatively

2. Describe a mural you have seen on a building or wall. What do you think is the purpose of the mural? **Accept reasonable responses.**

3. Think of a piece of art you have seen outside, such as a statue or sculpture. Describe it and tell whether or not you like it. Explain your reasons. **Accept reasonable responses.**

4. If you visited an art museum, what kinds of art would you expect to see there? How might the art inside the museum differ from art you might see outside at a park or in a public garden?
   Ideas: inside a museum: paintings, furniture, artifacts;
   outside: hardier, lasting sculptures

Word Meanings
Definitions
Look for these words as you read your chapter book. When you find one of these words, write its definition.

ancient: **having to do with times long past**
fresco: **a painting on freshly spread, moist plaster**
cattle: **cows, bulls, steers, and oxen, all of which are raised on farms and ranches**
polished: **a surface made bright or shiny**
sewing machine: **a machine with a motor that moves a needle and thread through fabric to make stitches**
umbrella: **a screen that is made of cloth or plastic stretched over a folding frame and held up by a stick; used to protect from rain or the sun**

Art for All!

Chapter Quiz

Name _____ Date _____

Art for All!
Chapter 1, "Public Art Rocks"
Fill in the bubble beside the answer for each question.

1. Public art is art that
   Ⓐ is created by the public.
   ● is displayed in a public place.
   Ⓒ stays inside a museum so the public can enjoy it for a very long time.

2. Cave art has been found in
   Ⓐ France and Spain.
   Ⓑ South America, India, and Africa.
   ● both A and B

3. Most cave paintings show
   ● animals.
   Ⓑ people doing daily work.
   Ⓒ objects people used long ago.

4. Why do many old rock paintings in Mexico still exist?
   Ⓐ People have protected the art.
   Ⓑ Artists have restored the paintings.
   ● The dry desert air has helped protect the paintings.

Read the question, and write your answer.

Why do you think people painted on cave walls? **Ideas: to teach children how to hunt; to leave records of the people's lives; to show off the artists' skills**

Art for All!

Chapter Quiz

Name _____ Date _____

Art for All!
Chapter 2, "Fresh Public Art"
Mark each statement *T* for true or *F* for false.

F 1. Diego Rivera was born in New Mexico.
F 2. Rivera wanted his murals to show poor people how wealthy people lived.
T 3. Rivera painted huge murals in cities across America.
T 4. Rivera's art led to an important mural movement.
F 5. There are still a lot of Rivera-style murals in the northeastern United States.
F 6. People have to know a lot about art to understand Rivera's murals.
F 7. Only a few cities have public art programs.
T 8. Albuquerque, New Mexico, has had a public art program for many years.
F 9. Some murals along the freeways in Miami-Dade, Florida, were painted for the 1984 Summer Olympic Games.
F 10. Public art programs are found only in the Southwest.

Read the question, and write your answer.

How did Rivera's murals help Mexican workers? **Rivera's murals show workers on farms and in cities; the murals encourage workers to be proud of their work.**

Art for All!

Chapter Quiz

Name _____ Date _____

Art for All!
Chapter 3, "Mural, Mural on the Wall"
Mark each statement *T* for true or *F* for false.

T 1. Women in Africa have painted murals on the walls of their homes for hundreds of years.
F 2. Most of the mural paintings in South Africa are still in homes.
F 3. Community murals are painted by city workers.
T 4. Like many of Rivera's murals, community murals show people working.
T 5. Some murals are used to teach people.
F 6. Community murals are also used to advertise businesses that serve people living in the community.
T 7. Some large murals are painted by artists who are paid for their work.
F 8. Paid artists are given strict instructions about what to paint.
F 9. Murals in South Africa often show black people separated from white people.
T 10. Murals reflect the important changes that have taken place in South Africa.

Read the question, and write your answer.

How are the murals in cities different from the murals women used to paint on their homes? **The murals women used to paint were mostly patterns; the murals on city walls show people, places, and changes in society.**

Art for All!

82   Express Yourself • Book 6

Answer Key

Chapter Quiz

Name _____ Date _____

Art for All!
Chapter 4, "The Wall"
Fill in the bubble beside the answer for each question.

1. The Vietnam Veterans Memorial is
   ● in a park, surrounded by trees and statues.
   Ⓑ a single, tall, black stone wall in Washington, D.C.
   Ⓒ located in a park in New York City.

2. The design by Maya Lin
   Ⓐ was chosen because it would be easy and inexpensive to build.
   Ⓑ finished third in the contest.
   ● was chosen from over 1,400 designs.

3. People who visit the Wall
   ● often leave items there.
   Ⓑ are not allowed to touch it.
   Ⓒ are allowed to use paper and pencils to make rubbings of the names on it.

4. Two other Vietnam War memorials have been added
   Ⓐ by people who were angry about the war.
   ● because some people did not like Lin's design.
   Ⓒ so more people would visit the memorial.

Read the question, and write your answer.
Where did the money to build the Wall come from? **companies, other groups, and nearly 300,000 Americans**

Express Yourself • Book 6   77

Art for All!

Chapter Quiz

Name _____ Date _____

Art for All!
Chapter 5, "The Public Says, 'No!'"
Mark each statement *T* for true or *F* for false.

__T__ 1. Richard Serra created a piece of art for a public place.
__T__ 2. Serra's art was part of a public art program in New York City.
__F__ 3. Most people really liked his work called *Tilted Arc*.
__F__ 4. *Tilted Arc* was a huge stone wall, 120 feet long, designed for Central Park.
__T__ 5. Some people said this piece of public art kept the public from using a public place.
__F__ 6. A private hearing on the artwork was held.
__T__ 7. The hearing ruled that the artwork should be removed.
__F__ 8. The artist was pleased to have his work moved to a new location.
__F__ 9. *Tilted Arc* was cut into pieces and moved to a private location.
__F__ 10. The artist's rights were more important than what people liked.

Read the question, and write your answer.
What were some of the complaints people had about *Tilted Arc*?
Ideas: Some people had to walk around the wall to get to work; some thought the wall was ugly; some complained that there was no place to sit.

78   Express Yourself • Book 6

Art for All!

Chapter Quiz

Name _____ Date _____

Art for All!
Chapter 6, "Miles of Public Art"
Fill in the bubble beside the answer for each question.

1. Christo and Jeanne-Claude Javacheff are
   Ⓐ public artists from Bolivia.
   Ⓑ public artists who live and work in Paris.
   ● two of the most famous public artists in the world.

2. Christo and Jeanne-Claude's public art creations
   Ⓐ take years to plan and last a long time.
   Ⓑ are often the same, but are displayed in different locations.
   ● take years to plan and are on display for a brief time.

3. Some of Christo and Jeanne-Claude's artwork involved
   Ⓐ wrapping thousands of small objects with orange fabric.
   ● wrapping a large building in Germany.
   Ⓒ building a wooden fence across more than 24 miles in California.

4. Who pays for the materials and workers needed for Christo and Jeanne-Claude's artwork?
   ● The artists pay for the cost of their artwork.
   Ⓑ Christo and Jeanne-Claude's artwork is part of a worldwide public art program.
   Ⓒ People pay to see the artwork.

Read the question, and write your answer.
Describe the kind of artwork created by Christo and Jeanne-Claude. What is the environmental impact of their displays? **Most of their work involves using fabric to change or draw attention to the landscape; their projects are massive in scale, but have no lasting environmental impact.**

Express Yourself • Book 6   79

Art for All!

Thinking and Writing

Name _____ Date _____

Art for All!
Think About It
Write about or give an oral presentation for each question.

1. How are Rivera's murals and community murals in South Africa similar? How are they different? **Both show how people live. Both are in public places. Murals in South Africa are painted by many different people. Rivera used a type of art called "fresco."**

2. How do people who visit the Vietnam Veterans Memorial interact with it? Do you think this is an important aspect of this memorial? Explain your answer. **Ideas: The Wall can be touched; people see themselves in the Wall. The listing of names makes the memorial personal.**

3. What aspects of *Tilted Arc* took away from its role as public art? **Ideas: It annoyed people because they had to walk around it; because it was made of steel, it rusted, and some people thought it was ugly; it did not make the public area enjoyable for people.**

4. Why do you think Christo and Jean-Claude only leave their work on display for about two weeks? **Accept reasonable responses.**

Write About It
Choose one of the questions below. Write your answer on a sheet of paper.

1. Why is public art important? How does it help people? How does it enrich our cities?

2. Write a letter to public officials in New York City asking that *Tilted Arc* be removed. In your letter, propose the type of art you would like to see in the Federal Plaza in New York.

3. If you were given the chance to choose Christo and Jeanne-Claude's next work of art, what would you suggest? Be specific and tell how it would be carried out.

4. Complete the Making Inferences Chart for this book.

80   Express Yourself • Book 6

Art for All!

Express Yourself • Book 6   83

Building Background

Name _____ Date _____

The Last Leaf and The Gift
What You Know

Write answers to these questions.

1. How does a short story differ from a novel? _____

2. Think about a time when you were sick and had to stay in bed. How did you pass the time? _____

3. Think about the setting of a story. Why is the setting so important in telling certain types of stories? _____
_____

4. What kinds of gifts can you give when you cannot afford to buy someone a special gift? _____

5. Think about life in the United States in 1900. List at least three things that were different then from now. _____

Word Meanings
Matching

Look for these words as you read your chapter book. When you find a word, draw a line to connect the word with the correct definition.

dough — a case of glass, paper, or other material that holds a light and protects it from wind and rain

dull — a printed collection of writing that comes out at a regular time and contains articles, stories, pictures, and various other kinds of information

fever — a disease in which the lungs become inflamed and a thin fluid collects in them

lantern — a body temperature that is higher than normal

magazine — a mixture of flour, water or milk, and other ingredients that is worked into a soft, thick mass and used to make baked goods

pneumonia — not bright; dim

Word Lists

The Last Leaf and The Gift

Unfamiliar Words	Word Meanings	Proper Nouns	
	original	Bay of Naples, Greenwich Village, Johnsy, New York City, O. Henry, South Carolina, Sue, Texas, William Porter	Chapter 1
	magazine		
broth, masterpiece, special	fever, pneumonia	California, Mr. Behrman	Chapter 2
	comb, lantern		Chapter 3
	anniversary, celebrate, married, dull	Della, Juan, Puerto Rico	Chapter 1
	leather, wrapped, dough		Chapter 2
	receive		Chapter 3

Express Yourself • Book 7

Chapter Quiz

Name _____ Date _____

The Last Leaf
Foreword and Chapter 1, "Greenwich Village"

Mark each statement *T* for true or *F* for false.

_____ 1. O. Henry was a well-known British writer.

_____ 2. Most people remember O. Henry for his full-length novels.

_____ 3. Greenwich Village is part of New York City.

_____ 4. Artists liked Greenwich Village because apartment rent was low.

_____ 5. Both Sue and Johnsy grew up in New York City.

_____ 6. Sue and Johnsy moved to Greenwich Village in late summer.

_____ 7. Sue and Johnsy lived in a building with many other artists.

_____ 8. Sue and Johnsy made pen and ink drawings for magazines.

_____ 9. Both Sue and Johnsy dreamed of becoming famous artists with their drawings in a lot of magazines.

_____ 10. Sue dreamed of painting the Bay of Naples.

Read the question, and write your answer.

Why did poor artists like the crooked streets of Greenwich Village?

_____

_____

_____

Chapter Quiz

Name _____ Date _____

The Last Leaf
Chapter 2, "The Visitor"

Number the events in order from 1 to 5.

____ Johnsy got pneumonia.

____ Sue found Johnsy looking out the window at a vine on the wall.

____ The doctor said Johnsy had a one in ten chance to live.

____ The season changed from summer to fall.

____ Johnsy said she would die when the last leaf fell from the vine.

Number the events in order from 6 to 10.

____ Sue went downstairs to get Mr. Behrman.

____ Sue closed the shade and heated broth for Johnsy.

____ Sue told Mr. Behrman about Johnsy and the vine.

____ Mr. Behrman left, muttering something about Johnsy.

____ Mr. Behrman sat for Sue to draw him.

Read the question, and write your answer.

What did Mr. Behrman want to paint? Why had he never painted it?

_____

_____

_____

Express Yourself • Book 7

Chapter Quiz

Name _____ Date _____

The Last Leaf
Chapter 3, "The Masterpiece"

Number the events in order from 1 to 5.

____ Johnsy talked about painting the Bay of Naples.

____ The second morning, the leaf was still on the vine.

____ When Sue opened the shade, there was only one leaf left on the vine.

____ Sue woke to the sound of wind and rain.

____ The one leaf stayed on the vine all day.

Mark each statement *T* for true or *F* for false.

____ 1. Seeing that the leaf stayed on the vine made Johnsy decide it was wrong to wish to die.

____ 2. Sue pulled the shade down each night so Johnsy could not see the vine.

____ 3. The doctor told Sue that Mr. Behrman was sick, but he thought Mr. Behrman would get better.

____ 4. Mr. Behrman got pneumonia because he could not afford to heat his apartment.

____ 5. Mr. Behrman stood in puddles of water to paint the leaf.

Read the question, and write your answer.

Why did Sue say the leaf was Mr. Behrman's masterpiece?

_____

_____

_____

Chapter Quiz

Name _____ Date _____

The Gift
Chapter 1, "Juan and Della"

Fill in the bubble beside the answer for each question.

1. Della was depressed and sad because she
   - Ⓐ did not have time to cook a special dinner for her husband.
   - Ⓑ did not have enough money to buy food for dinner.
   - Ⓒ only had $1.87.

2. Della needed money to buy her husband
   - Ⓐ a birthday gift.
   - Ⓑ an anniversary gift.
   - Ⓒ a new watch.

3. Della wanted to buy Juan a special gift because
   - Ⓐ she loved him so much.
   - Ⓑ he was giving her something nice.
   - Ⓒ he had lost his job.

4. Della was proud
   - Ⓐ of her job at the hotel.
   - Ⓑ because the couple earned enough to help support Juan's parents.
   - Ⓒ of her thick, black hair.

Read the question, and write your answer.

Why were Juan and Della so poor, even though they both worked?

_____

_____

_____

Express Yourself • Book 7   89

Chapter Quiz

Name _____ Date _____

The Gift
Chapter 2, "Della Finds a Way"

Number the events in order from 1 to 5.

____ Della went from shop to shop.

____ Della went to a store that sold hair goods.

____ When she found just the right thing, Della made her selection.

____ The woman at the store gave Della four crisp five-dollar bills.

____ The woman at the store cut off Della's hair.

Mark each statement *T* for true or *F* for false.

____ 1. Della chose a leather watchband because she knew it was the kind Juan liked most.

____ 2. After shopping, Della went straight home to fix dinner.

____ 3. Della curled her hair to make it look better.

____ 4. Della knew Juan would like her new haircut.

____ 5. For dinner, Della fixed meat pies.

Read the question, and write your answer.

Juan earned 20 dollars a week at his job. Compare this to the money Della got for her hair. How does this show her love for Juan?

_____

_____

_____

Chapter Quiz

Name _____ Date _____

The Gift
Chapter 3, "The Surprise"

Mark each statement *T* for true or *F* for false.

___ 1. Juan was often late getting home for dinner.

___ 2. When she heard Juan coming, Della was a little scared.

___ 3. Juan looked forward to having a family.

___ 4. Because he worked hard, Juan sometimes spent money on himself.

___ 5. When Juan saw Della's hair, he looked angry.

___ 6. Della told Juan she cut her hair because she was tired of it.

___ 7. Nothing could make Juan love his wife any less.

___ 8. Juan had bought Della a jeweled tiara for her hair.

___ 9. When Juan saw Della's gift to him, he smiled.

___ 10. Juan and Della were sad that they had wasted their money on these gifts.

Read the question, and write your answer.

How did Della and Juan each show, "It is better to give than to receive"?

_____

_____

_____

Express Yourself • Book 7   91

Thinking and Writing

Name _____ Date _____

The Last Leaf and The Gift
Think About It

Write about or give an oral presentation for each question.

1. Compare the gift Mr. Behrman gave Johnsy with the gifts Della and Juan gave each other. How are they alike? _____
_____

2. Compare the setting of "The Last Leaf" with the setting of "The Gift." In which story is the setting most important? Why?
_____

3. O. Henry wrote about the lives of common people. In these two stories, the people are poor. Why did Della and Juan need to be poor for "The Gift" to be a meaningful story? _____
_____

4. For each of the two stories, write a one-sentence summary of the surprise ending. _____
_____

Write About It

Choose one of the questions below. Write your answer on a sheet of paper.

1. Find out more about O. Henry, and write a two-page O. Henry-style story about his life.

2. Pretend you are Johnsy. Write a letter to your family telling about Mr. Behrman and his masterpiece.

3. Describe a special gift you would like to give to someone who has made a difference in your life.

4. Complete a Book Report Form for each of these stories.

Express Yourself • Book 7

Fluency Passages

The Last Leaf and The Gift

Chapter 2 *pages 8 and 9*

*"What are you doing, my friend?" Sue asked as she went over to the	14
bed to look out the window. There she saw a vine along the side of the	30
brick house next door. It was only 20 feet away. The cold weather had	44
stripped away many of its leaves.	50
"Six . . ." Johnsy whispered. "They are falling faster now. Three days	60
ago there were almost 100. It made my head hurt to count them. But now it	76
is easy. There goes another one. There are only five left now."	88
"Five what, dear? Tell me," Sue said.	95
"Leaves on the vine. When the last one falls, I must go too. I've	109
known that for three days. Didn't the doctor tell you?"	119
"Don't be silly. What do leaves have to do with you* getting well?"	132
Sue asked.	134

Chapter 2 *pages 32 and 33*

*She wanted a chain for Juan's special watch, because it did not have	13
a chain. Juan had to put the watch on a leather strap. Now the strap was old	30
and worn.	32
Yes, as soon as she saw it, Della knew that the gold chain must belong	47
to Juan. It was like him—simple yet grand. Juan was worth it, and it would	63
be her special anniversary gift to him.	70
Della smiled. She counted out 21 dollars and paid for the chain. She	83
still had 87 cents left. Della carefully wrapped the gold chain and stuck it	97
in her pocket. Then she took the subway to the hotel where she cleaned	111
rooms for a few hours.	116
Della held onto the special gift as she took the subway home before	129
dinner.*	130
When Della got into the apartment, she looked in the mirror.	141

- The target rate for **Express Yourself** is 130 wcpm. The asterisks (*) mark 130 words.

- Listen to the student read the passage. Count the number of words read in one minute and the number of errors.

- For the reading rate, subtract the number of errors from the total number of words read.

- Have students enter their scores on their **Fluency Graph.** See page 9.

Answer Key

Building Background

Name _____ Date _____

The Last Leaf and The Gift
What You Know
Write answers to these questions.

1. How does a short story differ from a novel? **A short story is shorter than a novel but still has characters, setting, and plot.**
2. Think about a time when you were sick and had to stay in bed. How did you pass the time? **Accept reasonable responses.**
3. Think about the setting of a story. Why is the setting so important in telling certain types of stories? **Ideas: gives the story a sense of place; helps the reader picture where the events are happening; helps the reader connect the story with real knowledge or experience**
4. What kinds of gifts can you give when you cannot afford to buy someone a special gift? **Accept reasonable responses.**
5. Think about life in the United States in 1900. List at least three things that were different then from now. **Ideas: lack of modern conveniences such as electricity, automobiles, airplanes, radio, television, computers, etc.**

Word Meanings
Matching

Look for these words as you read your chapter book. When you find a word, draw a line to connect the word with the correct definition.

- dough — a mixture of flour, water or milk, and other ingredients that is worked into a soft, thick mass and used to make baked goods
- dull — not bright; dim
- fever — a body temperature that is higher than normal
- lantern — a case of glass, paper, or other material that holds a light and protects it from wind and rain
- magazine — a printed collection of writing that comes out at a regular time and contains articles, stories, pictures, and various other kinds of information
- pneumonia — a disease in which the lungs become inflamed and a thin fluid collects in them

---

Chapter Quiz

Name _____ Date _____

The Last Leaf
Foreword and Chapter 1, "Greenwich Village"
Mark each statement *T* for true or *F* for false.

- **F** 1. O. Henry was a well-known British writer.
- **F** 2. Most people remember O. Henry for his full-length novels.
- **T** 3. Greenwich Village is part of New York City.
- **T** 4. Artists liked Greenwich Village because apartment rent was low.
- **F** 5. Both Sue and Johnsy grew up in New York City.
- **F** 6. Sue and Johnsy moved to Greenwich Village in late summer.
- **T** 7. Sue and Johnsy lived in a building with many other artists.
- **T** 8. Sue and Johnsy made pen and ink drawings for magazines.
- **F** 9. Both Sue and Johnsy dreamed of becoming famous artists with their drawings in a lot of magazines.
- **F** 10. Sue dreamed of painting the Bay of Naples.

Read the question, and write your answer.

Why did poor artists like the crooked streets of Greenwich Village? **The crooked streets and strange curves made it hard for people to find where the artists lived to collect money they owed.**

Chapter Quiz

Name _____ Date _____

The Last Leaf
Chapter 2, "The Visitor"
Number the events in order from 1 to 5.

- **2** Johnsy got pneumonia.
- **4** Sue found Johnsy looking out the window at a vine on the wall.
- **3** The doctor said Johnsy had a one in ten chance to live.
- **1** The season changed from summer to fall.
- **5** Johnsy said she would die when the last leaf fell from the vine.

Number the events in order from 6 to 10.

- **7** Sue went downstairs to get Mr. Behrman.
- **6** Sue closed the shade and heated broth for Johnsy.
- **8** Sue told Mr. Behrman about Johnsy and the vine.
- **10** Mr. Behrman left, muttering something about Johnsy.
- **9** Mr. Behrman sat for Sue to draw him.

Read the question, and write your answer.

What did Mr. Behrman want to paint? Why had he never painted it? **He wanted to paint a masterpiece but was afraid to begin.**

Chapter Quiz

Name _____ Date _____

The Last Leaf
Chapter 3, "The Masterpiece"
Number the events in order from 1 to 5.

- **5** Johnsy talked about painting the Bay of Naples.
- **4** The second morning, the leaf was still on the vine.
- **2** When Sue opened the shade, there was only one leaf left on the vine.
- **1** Sue woke to the sound of wind and rain.
- **3** The one leaf stayed on the vine all day.

Mark each statement *T* for true or *F* for false.

- **T** 1. Seeing that the leaf stayed on the vine made Johnsy decide it was wrong to wish to die.
- **T** 2. Sue pulled the shade down each night so Johnsy could not see the vine.
- **F** 3. The doctor told Sue that Mr. Behrman was sick, but he thought Mr. Behrman would get better.
- **F** 4. Mr. Behrman got pneumonia because he could not afford to heat his apartment.
- **F** 5. Mr. Behrman stood in puddles of water to paint the leaf.

Read the question, and write your answer.

Why did Sue say the leaf was Mr. Behrman's masterpiece? **Ideas: A masterpiece is a special painting for which people remember the artist; Sue and Johnsy would always remember Mr. Behrman for his painting of the leaf.**

---

94   Express Yourself • Book 7

Answer Key

Chapter Quiz

Name _____ Date _____

The Gift
Chapter 1, "Juan and Della"
Fill in the bubble beside the answer for each question.

1. Della was depressed and sad because she
   - Ⓐ did not have time to cook a special dinner for her husband.
   - Ⓑ did not have enough money to buy food for dinner.
   - ● only had $1.87.

2. Della needed money to buy her husband
   - Ⓐ a birthday gift.
   - ● an anniversary gift.
   - Ⓒ a new watch.

3. Della wanted to buy Juan a special gift because
   - ● she loved him so much.
   - Ⓑ he was giving her something nice.
   - Ⓒ he had lost his job.

4. Della was proud
   - Ⓐ of her job at the hotel.
   - Ⓑ because the couple earned enough to help support Juan's parents.
   - ● of her thick, black hair.

Read the question, and write your answer.

Why were Juan and Della so poor, even though they both worked?
Ideas: Apartment rent was high; they had to pay for water and heat and buy food and clothes; they sent money to Juan's parents; Juan's wages had been cut.

Chapter Quiz

Name _____ Date _____

The Gift
Chapter 2, "Della Finds a Way"
Number the events in order from 1 to 5.

- **4** Della went from shop to shop.
- **1** Della went to a store that sold hair goods.
- **5** When she found just the right thing, Della made her selection.
- **3** The woman at the store gave Della four crisp five-dollar bills.
- **2** The woman at the store cut off Della's hair.

Mark each statement T for true or F for false.

- **F** 1. Della chose a leather watchband because she knew it was the kind Juan liked most.
- **F** 2. After shopping, Della went straight home to fix dinner.
- **T** 3. Della curled her hair to make it look better.
- **F** 4. Della knew Juan would like her new haircut.
- **T** 5. For dinner, Della fixed meat pies.

Read the question, and write your answer.

Juan earned 20 dollars a week at his job. Compare this to the money Della got for her hair. How does this show her love for Juan?
Della was paid 20 dollars for her hair—as much money as Juan made in a week. Della happily spent the entire amount on a gift for Juan. This was an enormous amount, for this couple and for the time, to spend on an anniversary gift.

Chapter Quiz

Name _____ Date _____

The Gift
Chapter 3, "The Surprise"
Mark each statement T for true or F for false.

- **F** 1. Juan was often late getting home for dinner.
- **T** 2. When she heard Juan coming, Della was a little scared.
- **T** 3. Juan looked forward to having a family.
- **F** 4. Because he worked hard, Juan sometimes spent money on himself.
- **F** 5. When Juan saw Della's hair, he looked angry.
- **F** 6. Della told Juan she cut her hair because she was tired of it.
- **T** 7. Nothing could make Juan love his wife any less.
- **F** 8. Juan had bought Della a jeweled tiara for her hair.
- **T** 9. When Juan saw Della's gift to him, he smiled.
- **F** 10. Juan and Della were sad that they had wasted their money on these gifts.

Read the question, and write your answer.

How did Della and Juan each show, "It is better to give than to receive"?
Ideas: Each thought only of giving the perfect gift to the other; neither of them even thought about getting a gift in return.

Thinking and Writing

Name _____ Date _____

The Last Leaf and The Gift
Think About It

Write about or give an oral presentation for each question.

1. Compare the gift Mr. Behrman gave Johnsy with the gifts Della and Juan gave each other. How are they alike? **Ideas: Each gave unselfishly, focusing on the recipient of the gift.**

2. Compare the setting of "The Last Leaf" with the setting of "The Gift." In which story is the setting most important? Why?
   Answers will vary.

3. O. Henry wrote about the lives of common people. In these two stories, the people are poor. Why did Della and Juan need to be poor for "The Gift" to be a meaningful story? **With lots of money, neither would have needed to make a sacrifice.**

4. For each of the two stories, write a one-sentence summary of the surprise ending. **Accept reasonable responses.**

Write About It

Choose one of the questions below. Write your answer on a sheet of paper.

1. Find out more about O. Henry, and write a two-page O. Henry-style story about his life.

2. Pretend you are Johnsy. Write a letter to your family telling about Mr. Behrman and his masterpiece.

3. Describe a special gift you would like to give to someone who has made a difference in your life.

4. Complete a Book Report Form for each of these stories.

Express Yourself • Book 7   95

Building Background

Name _____ Date _____

Oliver Twist
What You Know

Write answers to these questions.

1. Why do you think the United States enacted and continues to enforce strict child labor laws? _____
_____

2. What is an orphan? What is an orphanage? _____
_____

3. Research the workhouse in England in the 1800s. Give a brief description and tell its purpose. _____
_____
_____
_____

Word Meanings
Definitions

Look for these words as you read your chapter book. When you find one of these words, write its definition.

alphabetical: _____

cruel: _____

funeral: _____

nephew: _____

stumble: _____

thief: _____

96   Express Yourself • Book 8

Word Lists

Oliver Twist

Unfamiliar Words	Word Meanings	Proper Nouns	
amazed bowl dreadful orphan soup workhouse	alphabetical	Mr. Bumble Mrs. Mann Oliver Twist	Chapter 1
buggy	funeral	Jack Dawkins London Mr. Sowerberry Noah	Chapter 2
actually beautiful	thief	Charlie Bates Fagin Mr. Brownlow Mrs. Bedwin	Chapter 3
terrible worst	cruel	Nancy Bill Sikes	Chapter 4
warn angry lantern niece stewards strength	stumble	Mr. Brittles Mr. Giles Mr. Monks Mrs. Maylie	Chapter 5
adopted amazing aunt married softhearted	nephew	Edwin Leeford West Indies	Chapter 6

Express Yourself • Book 8

97

Chapter Quiz

Name _____ Date _____

Oliver Twist
Chapter 1, "Born in a Workhouse"

Mark each statement *T* for true or *F* for false.

____ 1. Oliver Twist was born in Mrs. Mann's house.

____ 2. Oliver and his mother worked in the workhouse.

____ 3. Oliver lived with Mrs. Mann until he was nine.

____ 4. Oliver was happy and well cared for during the time he lived at Mrs. Mann's.

____ 5. Mr. Bumble ran the workhouse.

____ 6. Oliver was named after his father.

____ 7. Mr. Bumble wanted Oliver to help in the workhouse because Oliver was tall and strong.

____ 8. The boys picked Oliver to ask for more food.

____ 9. Oliver held out his plate and asked Mr. Bumble for more meat.

____ 10. Oliver was locked in a dark room for a week.

Read the question, and write your answer.

Why did Oliver live with Mrs. Mann? _____

_____

_____

Chapter Quiz

Name _____ Date _____

Oliver Twist
Chapter 2, "Oliver's First Job"

Fill in the bubble beside the answer for each question.

1. Oliver left the workhouse
   - Ⓐ because he was too old to stay there.
   - Ⓑ to work in a funeral home.
   - Ⓒ because he got into a fight with the other boys.

2. Noah was a bully who
   - Ⓐ said mean things about Oliver's mother.
   - Ⓑ picked on everybody.
   - Ⓒ was Mr. Sowerberry's son.

3. What happened after Oliver got into a fight with Noah?
   - Ⓐ Mr. Sowerberry sent Oliver to a workhouse in London.
   - Ⓑ Mr. Bumble took Oliver back to the workhouse.
   - Ⓒ Oliver ran away.

4. On the way to London,
   - Ⓐ Oliver was able to buy enough food to feed himself.
   - Ⓑ Oliver met many kind people who helped him.
   - Ⓒ Jack Dawkins found Oliver crying.

Read the question, and write your answer.

Why did Oliver think Jack was the strangest boy he had ever seen?

_____

_____

Express Yourself • Book 8

Chapter Quiz

Name _____ Date _____

Oliver Twist
Chapter 3, "Oliver in London"

Number the events in order from 1 to 5.

____ Oliver learned a new game from Fagin.

____ Oliver was arrested and taken to jail.

____ Jack and Charlie ran away.

____ Jack and Charlie robbed an old man.

____ Jack and Oliver walked the rest of the way to London.

Number the events in order from 6 to 10.

____ Mrs. Bedwin took care of Oliver.

____ Mr. Brownlow saw that Oliver looked like the lady in the painting.

____ The owner of the bookstore said Oliver was not the thief.

____ Oliver saw a painting in the bedroom.

____ Mr. Brownlow took Oliver home.

Read the question, and write your answer.

Why did Oliver keep looking at the painting in the bedroom?

_____

_____

_____

Chapter Quiz

Name _____ Date _____

Oliver Twist
Chapter 4, "Pulled Away"

Number the events in order from 1 to 5.

____ Nancy and Bill Sikes took Oliver back to Fagin.

____ Fagin sent Nancy to get Oliver.

____ Oliver asked Fagin to return the money to Mr. Brownlow.

____ Mr. Brownlow asked Oliver to take some money to the bookstore.

____ Nancy kept Fagin from hurting Oliver.

Mark each statement *T* for true or *F* for false.

____ 1. Mr. Bumble saw an ad placed in the paper by Mr. Brownlow.

____ 2. Mr. Bumble told Mr. Brownlow that Oliver was a hard worker.

____ 3. Mrs. Bedwin did not believe what Mr. Bumble said about Oliver.

____ 4. Mr. Brownlow did not believe that Oliver was a thief.

____ 5. Mr. Brownlow decided to tell the police that Oliver had disappeared.

Read the question, and write your answer.

Why do you think Mr. Brownlow's heart was broken?

_____

_____

_____

Express Yourself • Book 8

Chapter Quiz

Name _____ Date _____

Oliver Twist
Chapter 5, "Lost and Found"

Mark each statement *T* for true or *F* for false.

____ 1. Fagin needed a small boy to help him break into a house.

____ 2. Nancy warned Oliver about Bill.

____ 3. Oliver planned to go inside the house and warn the family.

____ 4. Stewards in the house frightened Oliver, and he dropped his lantern.

____ 5. An old nurse at the workhouse knew about Oliver's mother.

____ 6. After the break in, Bill left Oliver in the house and ran away.

____ 7. Oliver stumbled to a nearby house for help.

____ 8. The stewards did not recognize Oliver.

____ 9. Mrs. Maylie and her niece, Rose Maylie, were awakened by the stewards.

____ 10. Mrs. Maylie and her niece called the police.

Read the question, and write your answer.

What do you think will happen in the next chapter?

_____

_____

_____

Chapter Quiz

Name _____ Date _____

Oliver Twist
Chapter 6, "Home at Last"

Number the events in order from 1 to 5.

____ Oliver was sick for a long time.

____ The doctor came to treat Oliver.

____ The doctor took Oliver to Mr. Brownlow's house.

____ Mrs. Maylie and Miss Rose decided to help Oliver.

____ Oliver did not see Mr. Brownlow because he had moved away.

Mark each statement *T* for true or *F* for false.

____ 1. Oliver went to live in the country with Mrs. Maylie and Miss Rose.

____ 2. Fagin and Mr. Monks plotted to take Oliver.

____ 3. The woman in the painting was Oliver's aunt.

____ 4. Mrs. Maylie and Miss Rose adopted Oliver.

____ 5. Edwin Leeford was the father of both Oliver and Mr. Monks.

Read the question, and write your answer.

Why do you think Mr. Brownlow decided to find out what happened to the woman in the picture? _____

_____

Express Yourself • Book 8

Thinking and Writing

Name _____ Date _____

Oliver Twist
Think About It

Write about or give an oral presentation for each question.

1. Why do you think Oliver decided to stay at Fagin's house when he realized Fagin was a thief? _____
   _____

2. What were some of the things that happened to Oliver that seem unfair?
   _____
   _____

3. What was your favorite twist in this story? _____
   _____
   _____

4. Describe your favorite character in the story. Explain your choice.
   _____
   _____

Write About It
Choose one of the questions below. Write your answer on a sheet of paper.

1. Who do you think is the hero or heroine in this story? Who do you think is the villain? Explain your answer.

2. Create a police "Wanted" poster for either Fagin or Bill. Be sure to explain their crimes in your poster.

3. Do you think that being good is its own reward? Explain your answer.

4. Complete the Prediction/Outcome Chart for this book.

Fluency Passages

Oliver Twist

Chapter 2 *pages 8 and 9*

*Noah was much bigger than Oliver. So it was easy for Noah to tease	14
Oliver. He made Oliver do some of his work for him. He called Oliver	28
"Workhouse." Oliver was afraid to fight back. Noah picked on Oliver	39
every day, and Oliver did nothing to stop him. But one day, Noah said the	54
wrong thing.	56
"How's your mother, Workhouse?" Noah asked.	62
"She's dead," Oliver told him. "So don't you say anything about her!"	74
"What did she die of, Workhouse?" Noah said.	82
"Of a broken heart," Oliver said. "I think I know what it must be to	97
die of that!" A tear rolled down his cheek.	106
"What's making you cry now, Workhouse?" Noah asked.	114
"Not you," Oliver said. "Don't say anything more about my mother."	125
But Noah didn't stop. And* Oliver knew he wasn't going to stop.	137

Chapter 5 *pages 30 and 31*

*Now we must leave Oliver for a moment. I know you want to know	14
what has happened to him, but back at the workhouse, a very old nurse is	29
dying. She is important to our story. This woman had a lot of fun in her	45
life and did not mind dying. But she had something to say first.	58
"In this very room, I once nursed a pretty young lady," she said. "She	72
gave birth to a boy, and then she died. I took the only thing she had. It was	90
a gold locket.	93
"She had said the day would come when her baby boy would be glad	107
she was his mother," the dying nurse said.	115
"What was the boy's name?" the head nurse asked.	124
"They named him Oliver Twist."	129
And* what has happened to Oliver?	135

- The target rate for **Express Yourself** is 130 wcpm. The asterisks (*) mark 130 words.

- Listen to the student read the passage. Count the number of words read in one minute and the number of errors.

- For the reading rate, subtract the number of errors from the total number of words read.

- Have students enter their scores on their **Fluency Graph.** See page 9.

Answer Key

Building Background

Name _____ Date _____

Oliver Twist
What You Know
Write answers to these questions.

1. Why do you think the United States enacted and continues to enforce strict child labor laws? **Accept reasonable responses.**

2. What is an orphan? What is an orphanage? **An orphan is a child who has no parents; an orphanage is a home where orphans live.**

3. Research the workhouse in England in the 1800s. Give a brief description and tell its purpose. **The workhouse was a building where poor people were sent to live. Conditions were harsh to discourage people who were able to work from wanting to go there.**

Word Meanings
Definitions
Look for these words as you read your chapter book. When you find one of these words, write its definition.

alphabetical: **arranged in the regular order of the alphabet**
cruel: **having no mercy or pity; liking to make others suffer**
funeral: **the service held for a dead person**
nephew: **the son of one's brother or sister**
stumble: **to walk in an unsteady way**
thief: **a person who steals in a secret way**

96   Express Yourself • Book 8

Oliver Twist

Chapter Quiz

Name _____ Date _____

Oliver Twist
Chapter 1, "Born in a Workhouse"
Mark each statement *T* for true or *F* for false.

__F__ 1. Oliver Twist was born in Mrs. Mann's house.
__F__ 2. Oliver and his mother worked in the workhouse.
__T__ 3. Oliver lived with Mrs. Mann until he was nine.
__F__ 4. Oliver was happy and well cared for during the time he lived at Mrs. Mann's.
__T__ 5. Mr. Bumble ran the workhouse.
__F__ 6. Oliver was named after his father.
__F__ 7. Mr. Bumble wanted Oliver to help in the workhouse because Oliver was tall and strong.
__T__ 8. The boys picked Oliver to ask for more food.
__F__ 9. Oliver held out his plate and asked Mr. Bumble for more meat.
__T__ 10. Oliver was locked in a dark room for a week.

Read the question, and write your answer.

Why did Oliver live with Mrs. Mann? **Oliver's mother died after he was born. There was no one to take care of a baby in the workhouse.**

98   Express Yourself • Book 8

Oliver Twist

Chapter Quiz

Name _____ Date _____

Oliver Twist
Chapter 2, "Oliver's First Job"
Fill in the bubble beside the answer for each question.

1. Oliver left the workhouse
   Ⓐ because he was too old to stay there.
   ● to work in a funeral home.
   Ⓒ because he got into a fight with the other boys.

2. Noah was a bully who
   ● said mean things about Oliver's mother.
   Ⓑ picked on everybody.
   Ⓒ was Mr. Sowerberry's son.

3. What happened after Oliver got into a fight with Noah?
   Ⓐ Mr. Sowerberry sent Oliver to a workhouse in London.
   Ⓑ Mr. Bumble took Oliver back to the workhouse.
   ● Oliver ran away.

4. On the way to London,
   Ⓐ Oliver was able to buy enough food to feed himself.
   Ⓑ Oliver met many kind people who helped him.
   ● Jack Dawkins found Oliver crying.

Read the question, and write your answer.

Why did Oliver think Jack was the strangest boy he had ever seen? **Jack was short, had crooked legs, walked and talked like a grown man, and wore a man's coat that was too big for him.**

Express Yourself • Book 8   99

Oliver Twist

Chapter Quiz

Name _____ Date _____

Oliver Twist
Chapter 3, "Oliver in London"
Number the events in order from 1 to 5.

__2__ Oliver learned a new game from Fagin.
__5__ Oliver was arrested and taken to jail.
__4__ Jack and Charlie ran away.
__3__ Jack and Charlie robbed an old man.
__1__ Jack and Oliver walked the rest of the way to London.

Number the events in order from 6 to 10.

__8__ Mrs. Bedwin took care of Oliver.
__10__ Mr. Brownlow saw that Oliver looked like the lady in the painting.
__6__ The owner of the bookstore said Oliver was not the thief.
__9__ Oliver saw a painting in the bedroom.
__7__ Mr. Brownlow took Oliver home.

Read the question, and write your answer.

Why did Oliver keep looking at the painting in the bedroom? **Oliver thought the woman looked beautiful and kind, and the eyes of the lady seemed to be looking at him.**

100   Express Yourself • Book 8

Oliver Twist

---

106   Express Yourself • Book 8

Answer Key

Chapter Quiz

Name _____ Date _____

Oliver Twist
Chapter 4, "Pulled Away"
Number the events in order from 1 to 5.

_3_ Nancy and Bill Sikes took Oliver back to Fagin.
_1_ Fagin sent Nancy to get Oliver.
_4_ Oliver asked Fagin to return the money to Mr. Brownlow.
_2_ Mr. Brownlow asked Oliver to take some money to the bookstore.
_5_ Nancy kept Fagin from hurting Oliver.

Mark each statement *T* for true or *F* for false.

_T_ 1. Mr. Bumble saw an ad placed in the paper by Mr. Brownlow.
_F_ 2. Mr. Bumble told Mr. Brownlow that Oliver was a hard worker.
_T_ 3. Mrs. Bedwin did not believe what Mr. Bumble said about Oliver.
_F_ 4. Mr. Brownlow did not believe that Oliver was a thief.
_F_ 5. Mr. Brownlow decided to tell the police that Oliver had disappeared.

Read the question, and write your answer.
Why do you think Mr. Brownlow's heart was broken?
Mr. Brownlow had been very kind to Oliver, but now he believed Oliver was a fake and a thief.

Express Yourself • Book 8   101

Oliver Twist

Chapter Quiz

Name _____ Date _____

Oliver Twist
Chapter 5, "Lost and Found"
Mark each statement *T* for true or *F* for false.

_F_ 1. Fagin needed a small boy to help him break into a house.
_T_ 2. Nancy warned Oliver about Bill.
_T_ 3. Oliver planned to go inside the house and warn the family.
_T_ 4. Stewards in the house frightened Oliver, and he dropped his lantern.
_T_ 5. An old nurse at the workhouse knew about Oliver's mother.
_F_ 6. After the break in, Bill left Oliver in the house and ran away.
_F_ 7. Oliver stumbled to a nearby house for help.
_F_ 8. The stewards did not recognize Oliver.
_T_ 9. Mrs. Maylie and her niece, Rose Maylie, were awakened by the stewards.
_F_ 10. Mrs. Maylie and her niece called the police.

Read the question, and write your answer.
What do you think will happen in the next chapter?
Accept reasonable responses.

102   Express Yourself • Book 8

Oliver Twist

Chapter Quiz

Name _____ Date _____

Oliver Twist
Chapter 6, "Home at Last"
Number the events in order from 1 to 5.

_3_ Oliver was sick for a long time.
_1_ The doctor came to treat Oliver.
_4_ The doctor took Oliver to Mr. Brownlow's house.
_2_ Mrs. Maylie and Miss Rose decided to help Oliver.
_5_ Oliver did not see Mr. Brownlow because he had moved away.

Mark each statement *T* for true or *F* for false.

_T_ 1. Oliver went to live in the country with Mrs. Maylie and Miss Rose.
_T_ 2. Fagin and Mr. Monks plotted to take Oliver.
_F_ 3. The woman in the painting was Oliver's aunt.
_F_ 4. Mrs. Maylie and Miss Rose adopted Oliver.
_T_ 5. Edwin Leeford was the father of both Oliver and Mr. Monks.

Read the question, and write your answer.
Why do you think Mr. Brownlow decided to find out what happened to the woman in the picture? **He guessed that the woman was Oliver's mother, and he still wanted to help Oliver.**

Express Yourself • Book 8   103

Oliver Twist

Thinking and Writing

Name _____ Date _____

Oliver Twist
Think About It
Write about or give an oral presentation for each question.

1. Why do you think Oliver decided to stay at Fagin's house when he realized Fagin was a thief? **Accept reasonable responses.**

2. What were some of the things that happened to Oliver that seem unfair?
Ideas: Jack and Charlie were pickpockets, but Oliver got caught; Mr. Brownlow thought Oliver had left with his money, but Nancy and Bill had grabbed Oliver.

3. What was your favorite twist in this story? **Ideas: Oliver's mother was the second wife of Mr. Brownlow's best friend; Miss Rose was the sister of Oliver's mother.**

4. Describe your favorite character in the story. Explain your choice.
Accept reasonable responses.

Write About It
Choose one of the questions below. Write your answer on a sheet of paper.

1. Who do you think is the hero or heroine in this story? Who do you think is the villain? Explain your answer.
2. Create a police "Wanted" poster for either Fagin or Bill. Be sure to explain their crimes in your poster.
3. Do you think that being good is its own reward? Explain your answer.
4. Complete the Prediction/Outcome Chart for this book.

104   Express Yourself • Book 8

Oliver Twist

Express Yourself • Book 8   107

Graphic Organizer

Name _____ Date _____

Thousand-Mile Words
Cause and Effect Chart

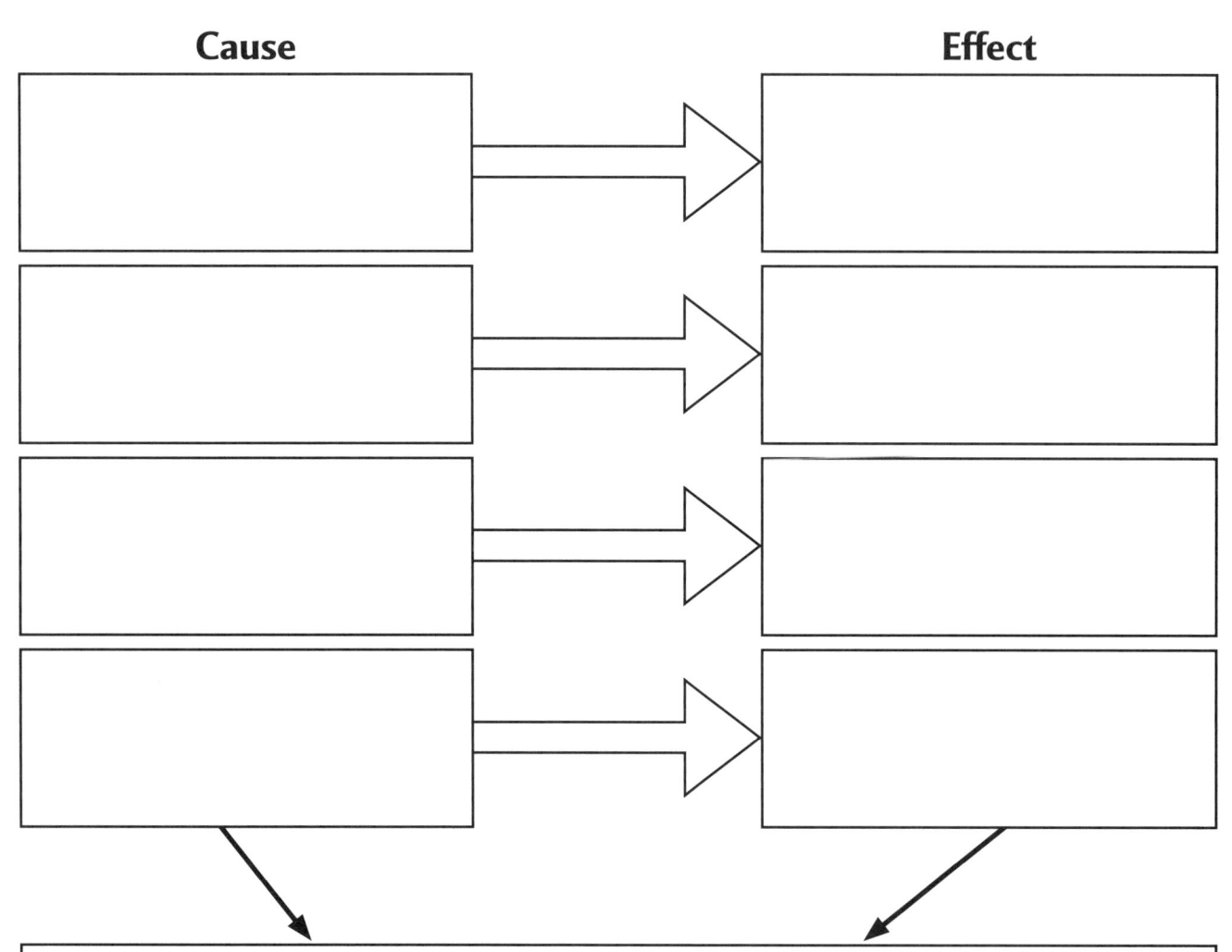

Cause → **Effect**

- Explain how you think Tino's experiences in the book change his attitude and make him a "different" person.
- Do you think Tino is a better person for the changes he makes? Why or why not?

Express Yourself

Graphic Organizer

Name _____ Date _____

They Landed One Night
Genres Chart

Reality (fact)	Fantasy (fiction)

Express Yourself

Graphic Organizer

Name _____ Date _____

Bidding on the Past
Main Idea/Details Chart

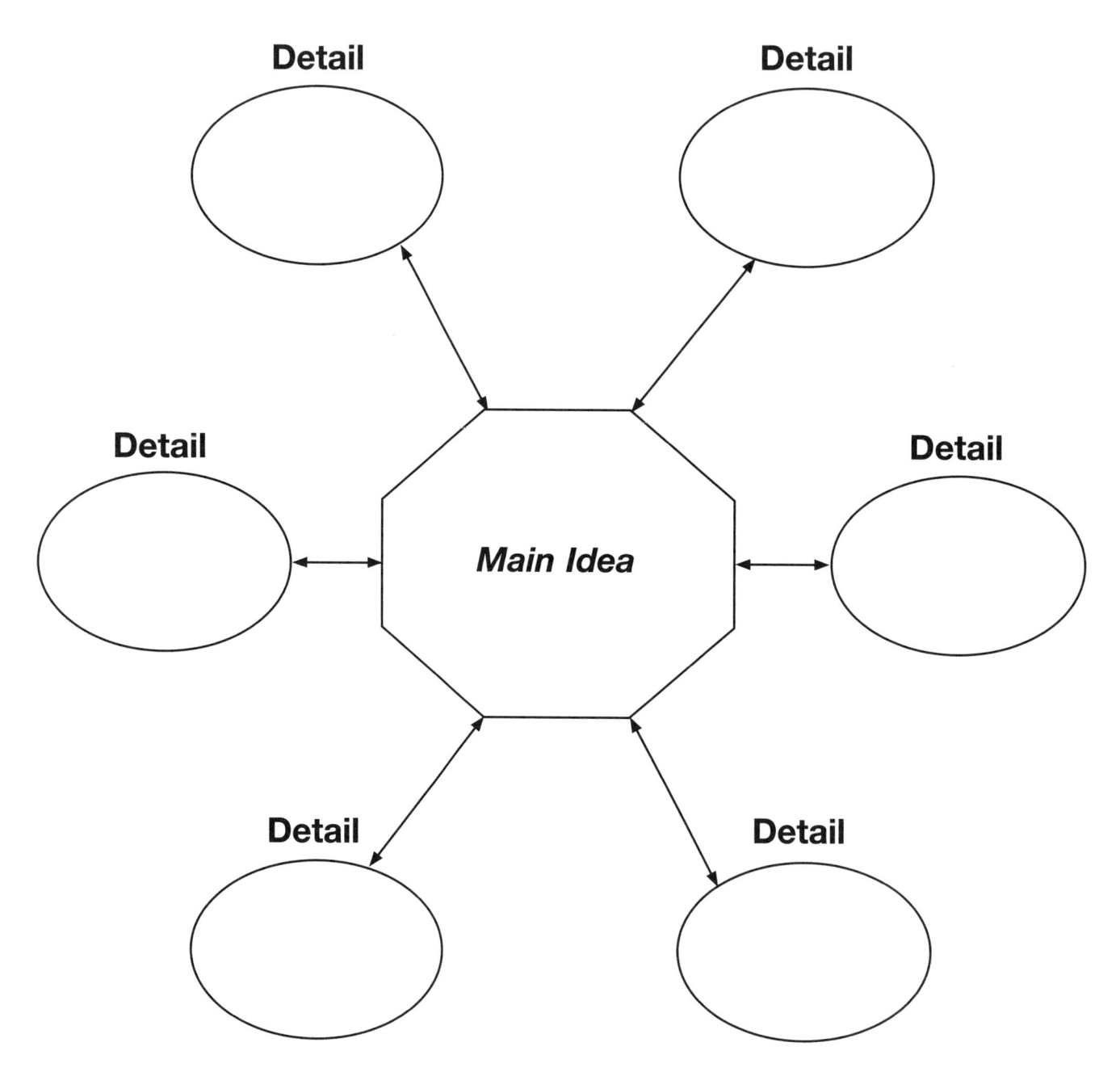

Detail

Detail

Detail

Main Idea

Detail

Detail

Detail

Express Yourself

Graphic Organizer

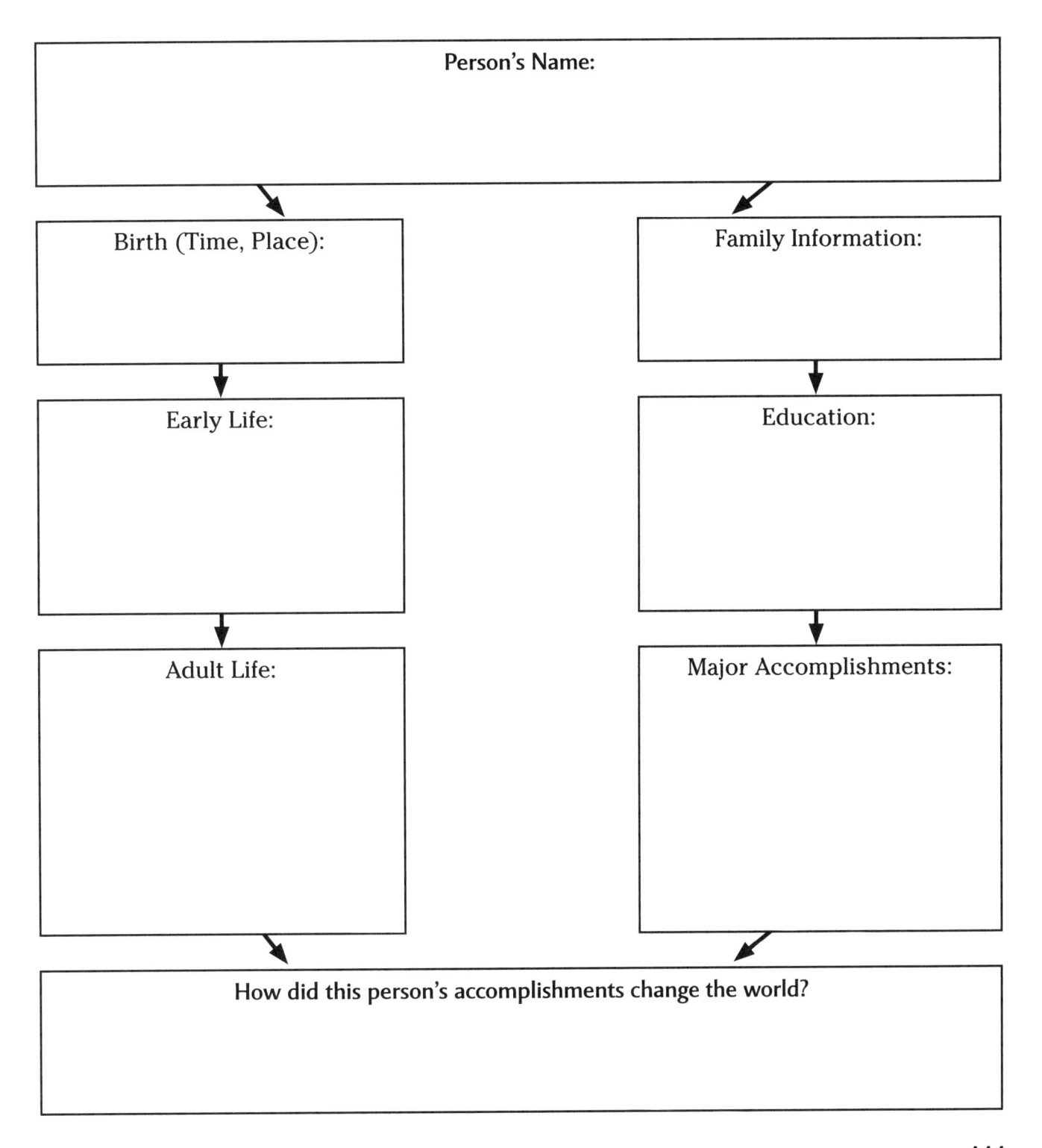

Name _____ Date _____

Blues King: The Story of B. B. King
Book Report Form

Person's Name:

Birth (Time, Place):

Family Information:

Early Life:

Education:

Adult Life:

Major Accomplishments:

How did this person's accomplishments change the world?

Express Yourself

Graphic Organizer

Name _____ Date _____

Sports Superstars
Compare and Contrast Chart

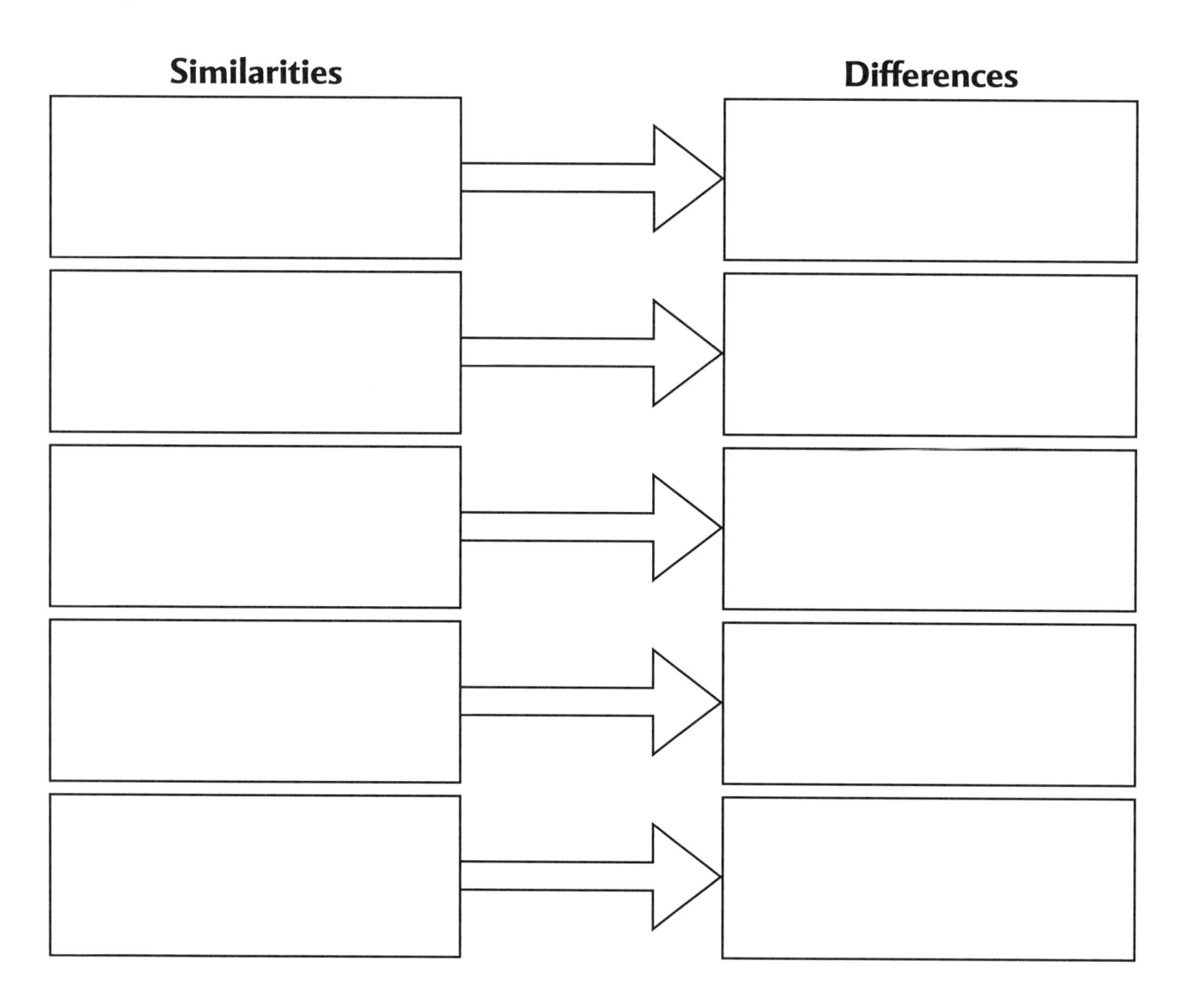

Similarities   **Differences**

Express Yourself

Name _____ Date _____

Art for All!
Making Inferences Chart

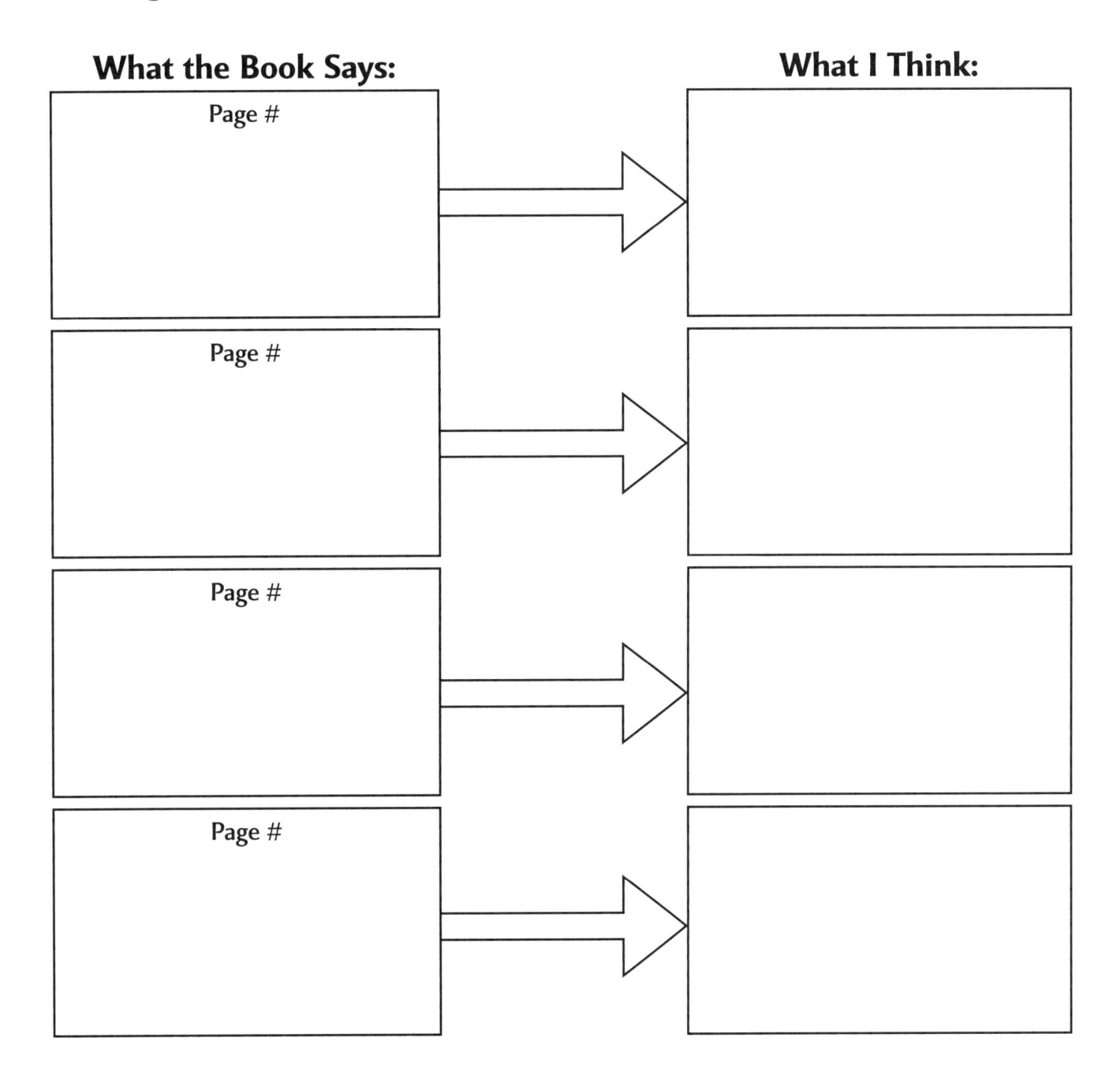

What the Book Says:

Page #

Page #

Page #

Page #

What I Think:

Express Yourself

Graphic Organizer

Name _____ Date _____

The Last Leaf and The Gift
Book Report Form

On lines 1–4, list the major plot events. On line 5, write the turning point or climax of the conflict. On line 6, write the falling action. On line 7, write how the story ended.

1. _____

2. _____

3. _____

4. _____

Rising Action

Climax

5. _____

Falling Action

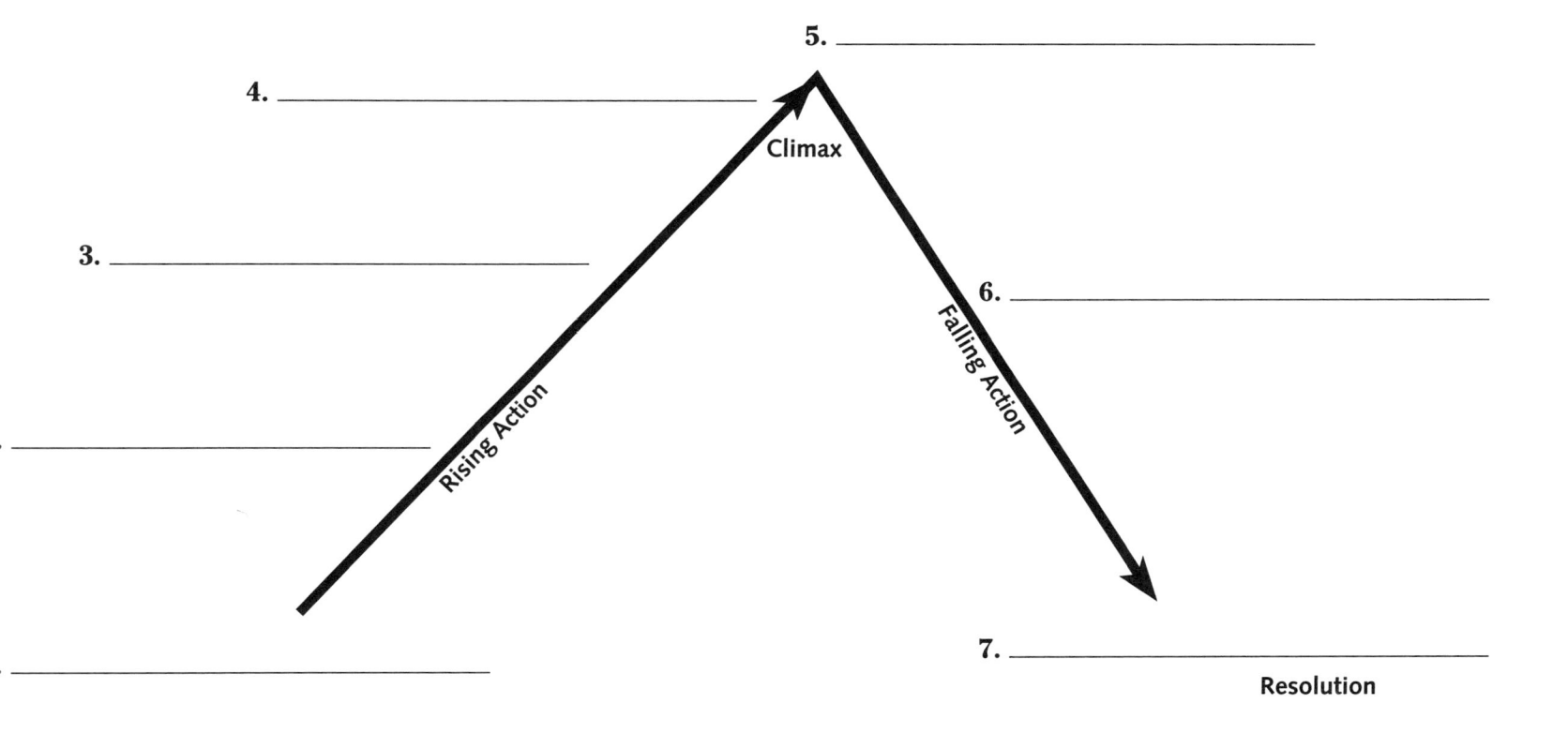

6. _____

7. _____

Resolution

Graphic Organizer

Name _____ Date _____

Oliver Twist
Prediction/Outcome Chart

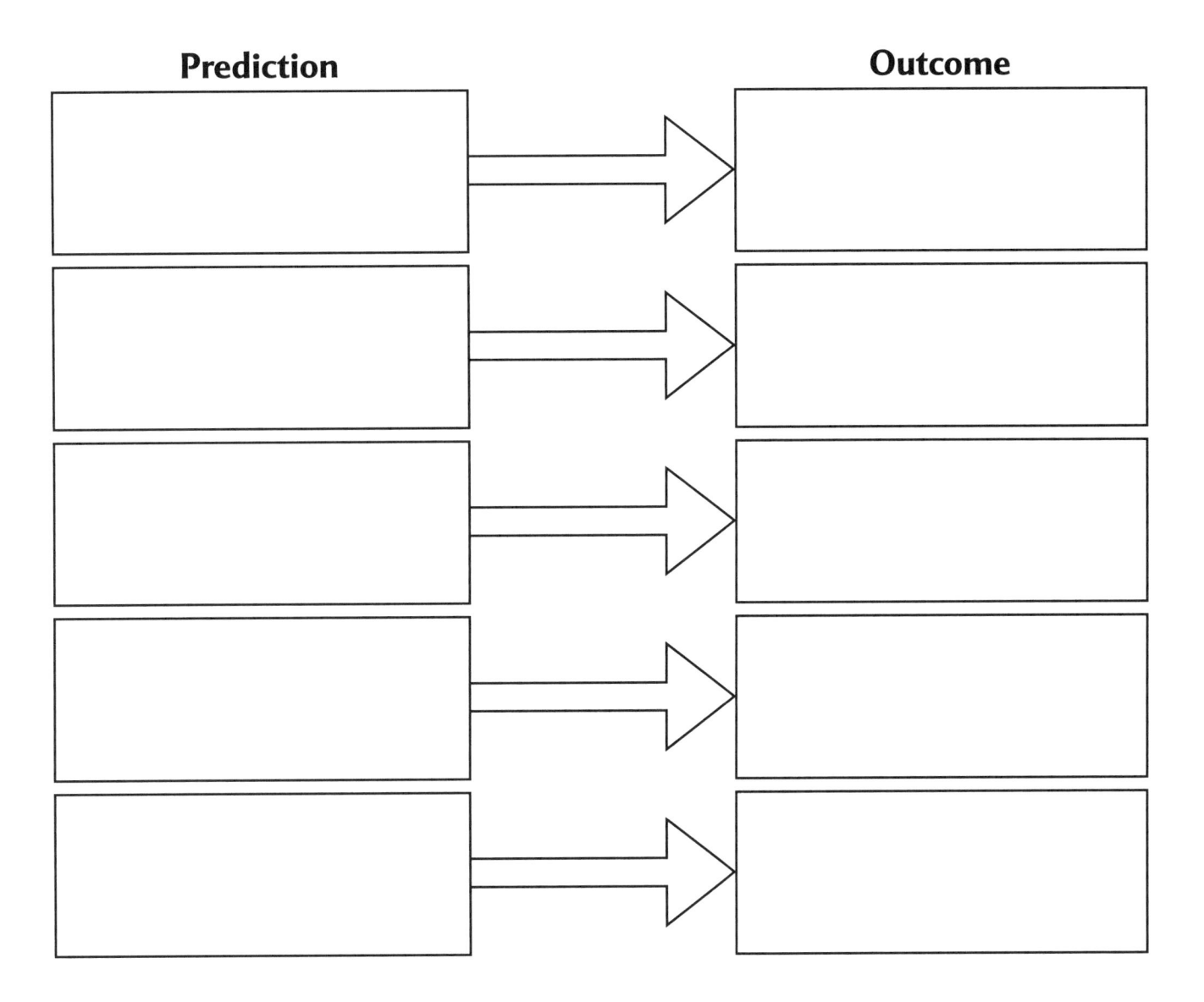

Prediction → **Outcome**

Express Yourself

115